GRACE UPON GRACE
A Collection of Sermons

David Johnson

This is a collection of sermons preached at Christ Episcopal Church in Charlottesville, Virginia by the Rev. Dr. David Johnson. The sermons do not now, nor have ever had any connection, affiliation, or sponsorship with any of the author(s), artist(s) or publications quoted or referenced herein. The content is intended for the purpose of commentary, study, discussion, literary and religious critique.

GRACE UPON GRACE

Published by David Johnson
Copyright © 2012 by David Johnson

First Printing: December, 2012
Printed in the United States of America

First Edition: May, 2012

ISBN-13: 978-1481181440

ISBN-10: 1481181440

Dedicated with gratitude and affection to my family and to Christ Episcopal Church, Charlottesville.

ACKNOWLEDGEMENTS

This book would not have been possible without the help of several people.

Special thanks to Paul Walker, Rector of Christ Episcopal Church, Charlottesville and without question one of the most gifted preachers and pastors I know, as well as a close friend. His encouragement and support in this project is greatly appreciated.

Thanks too to Ethan Richardson, another close friend as well as an exceptionally gifted writer. His creativity, eye for detail, and skill with formatting and language were an enormous help.

Thanks too to Will McDavid and Mary Boyce Hicks, two other close friends who did an outstanding job with the final formatting of this book.

Thanks to the staff and congregation of Christ Episcopal Church, Charlottesville, Virginia—the kindness, appreciation, and generosity you give me week in and week out continue to show me what the grace of God looks like—what a joy and privilege to serve and worship with you.

Finally, thanks to my family—I love you more than you know.

CONTENTS

PREFACE   11
From the Reverend Paul N. Walker

INTRODUCTION   13

I HAVE LOVED YOU   15
Why We Never Tire of Silly Love Songs

MERCY TRIUMPHS OVER JUDGMENT   23
Pageants, Pensions, and the Gospel Lens Cap

GOD IS ON YOUR SIDE   31
Songs for the Road of Despair

HIS GRACE IS ENOUGH   39
Bad Teachers, Chalkboards, and the Only Lesson that Matters

GETTING OVER YOURSELF   47
The Baptismal Death to Self-Reliance

THE WINE OF GRACE   55
The Only Way Out for a Dead Batmobile

HAVE MERCY ON ME, O GOD   63
Lenten Disciplines, Confession, and the Cry for Help

GOD IS A RESTORING GOD   71
Charcoal Fires and the Brand New Start

JUSTIFIED BY FAITH   79
Why Nuns and Trashcans Never Worked for Springsteen

DISTRACTED   87
Mary, Martha and the Better Portion

GOD HAS PAID FOR EVERYTHING   97
Shakey's Pizza Parlor and the Chop Shop Hero

GOD IS MERCIFUL TO SINNERS   105
Marlo Thomas and the Only Acceptance Letter You'll Ever Need

A CHANCE TO LIVE AGAIN   113
The Clarence Effect and the Power of Repentance

GOD IS FAITHFUL   121
Love from the Roller Rink

THE ELEVATOR DOOR IS ALWAYS OPEN   129
Old Wounds and God's Reconciling Love

WHY HAVE YOU FORSAKEN ME?   137
"Cowper's Grave" and the Shared Loneliness of God

ONCE FOR ALL   143
Derek Jeter's Extra-Innings Birthday Present

NO TAKE-BACKS   153
T.S. Eliot and the Irrevocable Hostess Cupcake

SCRAMBLING TO BE FIRST   159
Christ's Freedom in the Rat Race

THE GENTLENESS OF JESUS CHRIST   169
McFly's Solace in a World of Biffs

GOD'S DESTINY FOR YOU   179
What It Means When It Doesn't Go the Way You Thought It Should

GOD OUR COMFORTER 187
Love in the Age of Credit Card Debt

MOVED WITH PITY 197
The Don Johnson We Want To Be and the Valentine Who Did All the Choosing

GOD SENT HIS SON TO SAVE THE WORLD 205
Rip Tides, Friendship Bracelets, and Nicodemus' Gospel Train

WHAT LOVE THE FATHER HAS GIVEN US 215
Coors Light and the Ministry of Substitution

THE VALLEY OF THE SHADOW OF DEATH 225
Independence, Wilderness, and Our Hour of Darkness

NO GREATER LOVE 235
Letting a Mother off the Hook

THE SPIRIT HELPS US IN WEAKNESS 245
Paul Simon and the Paraclete

BEYOND ALL MEASURE 253
Impossible Grief and the Eternal Weight of Glory

EVERYTHING HAS BECOME NEW 263
Of Earthly Fathers and a Heavenly Father

THE WAY OF GRACE 273
Unfulfilled Callings, Motivational Posters, and that Old Love

PREFACE

If you are in need of a word of grace, you have come to the right place.

The sermons in this powerful collection are enveloping reminders of God's inexhaustible storehouse of grace. With care and skill, the Reverend Dr. David Johnson rummages through all stratospheres of culture—music, movies, television, history and literature—to deliver compelling messages of rest for the weary and strength for the weak.

The sermons in *Grace upon Grace* ring true to life because they have emerged out of the preacher's life. You will not find "sermonizing" here in the pejorative sense. You will find gift after gift offered from Dr. Johnson's seamless intermingling of scripture and schooldays, theater and theology, wisdom and wit emerging from his own human (and therefore, broken) experience. You will find a voice that will come along side of you and say, *"all shall be well, and all manner of things shall be well."*

So whether you read this collection one sermon at a time, or if you discover that you cannot put down the addictive gospel of grace, you are certain to experience what Prayer Book architect Thomas Cranmer called the *"increase of true religion."* For that, people of all sorts and conditions can sigh a collective "amen."

The Reverend Paul N. Walker
Rector, Christ Episcopal Church
Charlottesville, VA

INTRODUCTION

*From his fullness we have all received, grace
upon grace (John 1:16).*

This book is a collection of some of the sermons I have preached over the past several years at Christ Episcopal Church, Charlottesville, Virginia. The heart of what we preach at Christ Church is the grace of God because the grace of God is the heart of the gospel. The grace of God given us in Jesus Christ is good news for sinners, which includes all of us, and is the common thread that runs through every sermon preached at Christ Church, including those in this book.

In the prologue of his account of the gospel John puts it this way: "From his fullness we have all received, *grace upon grace*" (John 1:16). The Apostle Paul also emphasizes the grace of God: "For *by grace* you have been saved through faith, and this is not your own doing; it is the gift of God" (Ephesians 2:8). The ultimate demonstration of the grace of God toward sinners is the death of Jesus Christ on the cross, that as the Apostle Paul writes to the Romans: "God proves his love for us in that while we still were sinners Christ died for us" (Romans 5:8).

The grace of God has changed my life again and again. The grace of God brings comfort, relief, forgiveness, and encouragement. My hope is that this book will remind you that regardless of the never-ending changes in your life, the grace of God toward you has never and will never change, that God loves you all the time no matter what.

I HAVE LOVED YOU
Why We Never Tire of Silly Love Songs

As the Father has loved me, so I have loved you; abide in my love. If you keep my commandments, you will abide in my love, just as I have kept my Father's commandments and abide in his love. I have said these things to you so that my joy may be in you, and that your joy may be complete. This is my commandment, that you love one another as I have loved you (John 15:9-12).

In the Name of the Father, Son, and Holy Spirit.

One of my favorite TV shows is *The Office*. The show features a dysfunctional regional office of a mid-Atlantic paper company. The manager is Michael Scott, played by Steve Carell. Often the characters give mini interviews to give the show a documentary feel. In one of these interviews Michael describes how he related to his father: "I hate it when people don't tell each other why they're angry. My dad was like that. I would say, 'What's wrong, Dad? What's wrong, Dad? What's wrong, Dad? What's wrong, Dad?' over and over and over and he would just look at me like I was an idiot."

This morning's Gospel lesson from John 15 comes from Jesus' discourse at the Last Supper. It was the final time he spoke freely with his disciples before his passion and death. It is at the Last Supper that he pours out his heart to his disciples and gives them the bottom line. And in this morning's Gospel lesson Jesus repeats a simple phrase: "I have loved you." In 15:9 Jesus says, "As the Father has loved me, so *I have loved you*" and then in 15:12 he says, "This is my commandment, that you love one another as *I have loved you.*"

When I was a kid one of my favorite bands was Wings, the band Paul McCartney assembled and led in the years after The Beatles. One of their biggest hits was called "Silly Love Songs." Listen to these lyrics:

> You'd think that people would have had enough of
>   silly love songs.
> But I look around me and I see it isn't so.
> Some people wanna fill the world withsilly love
>   songs.
> And what's wrong with that?
> I'd like to know, 'cause here I go again
> I love you, I love you, I love you, I love you.

We don't ever really tire of silly love songs because we perpetually need to be reminded that we are loved. It's common that when my two youngest kids go to bed at night the last words go something like this: "Goodnight. *Goodnight.* I love you. *Love you too.* See you in the morning. *Okay.* I love you. *Love you too.* Get good sleep. *You too.* I love you. *Love you too.*" I'm not exaggerating—that's how it really goes, and it matters a lot. We need being reminded that we love each other.

Jesus knows that it matters a lot, and so at the Last Supper he reminds his disciples multiple times of his love for them. Yet in this gospel lesson Jesus does not say "I love you," to the disciples, but rather "I *have* loved you."

In other words, Jesus has always loved you, Jesus loves you right now, and Jesus will always love you.

Jesus has always loved you. Just think. Jesus has loved you from before you were born, before you were a glint in your parents' eyes, before time itself. Jesus has loved you in the good times. He loved you when you were born, when you learned to walk, when you learned to eat, when your parents read you *Goodnight Moon*. He loved you on your first day of school, when you had your first crush, when you passed the class you thought you'd never pass. Jesus loved you when you played your first chord on the piano, when you learned how to hit a baseball or ride a bike. Jesus loved you when you ate your first banana split, got your driver's license, went on your first date.

Jesus has loved you in the hard times. He loved you when you got made fun of at school, when your parents fought and you got a knot in your stomach, when the family pet died, when the family was too busy with other things to spend time with you. He loved you when you had your heart broken, when you got in trouble, when you made the biggest mistakes in your life. Jesus loved you when others hurt you, when the minister laid guilt trips on you. Jesus has loved you when you couldn't stop, even when it reached addiction. Jesus has *always* loved you.

Jesus loves you because God the Father loves Jesus. Listen to what Jesus said in this morning's Gospel lesson, "As the Father has loved me, so I have loved you."

God the Father loved Jesus from all eternity, when he created the heavens and the earth and people and everything through Jesus Christ. God the Father loved Jesus when he was rejected as illegitimate while still in his mother Mary's womb, when he was born in a barn, when he was blowing the minds of the rabbis in the temple as a twelve-year old. At Jesus' baptism God the Father spoke out of heaven, "This is my Beloved Son, with whom I am well-pleased." At the Mount of Transfiguration God the Father spoke again from heaven, "This is my Beloved Son, with whom I am well-pleased."

God the Father loved Jesus when he called the disciples, when he fed the five thousand, when he walked on water, when he raised Lazarus from the dead, when he spoke to the woman at the well, when he healed lepers no one else would touch. God the Father loved Jesus when he was betrayed, mocked, beaten, accused of things he didn't do, spit on, stripped, nailed on a cross and left to die. God the Father loved Jesus when he felt forsaken. God the Father loved Jesus as he died on the cross for you and me. And in the same way Jesus wept when Lazarus died, God the Father wept when his Son, Jesus, died—and the heavens opened up and his tears flooded down.

And God the Father loved Jesus when he raised him on the third day, when Jesus walked on the Emmaus Road, when Jesus comforted his frightened disciples, when Jesus ascended into heaven. And God the Father loves Jesus right now as he is seated at his right hand in heaven.

And because God the Father loves Jesus right now, Jesus loves you right now as well. He loves you right now, in the midst of the things that excite you, hurt you, scare you, fascinate you. He loves you right now, in the midst of all the things that keep you up at night, make you tense in your back and neck, remind you that you are not nearly as in control of things as you think you are.

Jesus loves you right now, in the midst of the skeletons in your closet, the hurts you tell no one about, the temptations you face every single day. Jesus loves you right now, in the midst of the hopes and dreams and goals and ambitions and desires and plans that animate you. Jesus loves you in the midst of your doubt and cynicism. When you don't care if he loves you, Jesus loves you anyway.

Jesus has always loved you because God the Father has always loved Jesus, as he told his disciples, "As the Father has loved me, so I have loved you."

Jesus has always loved you. Jesus loves you now. Jesus will always love you.

Jesus will love you as you grow up and grow old. He will love you when you get into the college or grad school you want to attend, he will love you when you get the "We regret to inform you..." letter. He will love you if you get married, if you stay married, if you don't stay married, if you never get married. He will love you if you have kids and grandkids, if you do not have kids or grandkids, or if, tragically, you outlive your kids or grandkids. He will love you when you're old, when you outlive your closest friends, when your health fails, when your savings dwindle, when you deal with the realities and fears of end of life issues, when you feel alone on death's doorstep.

He will love you when he welcomes you into heaven and wipes every tear from your eyes, when you are reunited with loved ones, when you join the millions upon millions of other people that Jesus has always loved, loves now, and will always love—and there you will be able to worship and thank him forever.

The ultimate proof that Jesus has always loved us, loves us now, and will love us forever is his death on the cross for our sins. In today's Gospel passage Jesus told the disciples at the Last Supper, "No one has greater love than this, to lay down one's life for one's friends." The very next day he did just that for us as he willingly lay down his life on the cross, as the Apostle Paul wrote in his Letter to the Romans, "God proves his love for us in that while we were still sinners Christ died for us" (5:8).

And out of gratitude for the fact that Jesus has always loved us, loves us now, and will always love us we are called to love others. In this morning's Gospel lesson Jesus said, "This is my commandment, that you love one another as I have loved you." Or as the Apostle John wrote in his first letter, "We know love by this, that (Jesus) laid down his life for us—and we ought to lay down our lives for one another" (1 John 3:16).

One of the most powerful films I've ever seen is *Saving Private Ryan* from 1998. The film opens with an elderly James Ryan returning with his family to Normandy to visit the grave of Captain John Miller, who had literally given his life to save him. The film portrays all that Miller and the other soldiers went through in order to save Private Ryan. Then the movie concludes with the elderly James Ryan falling down in gratitude at the grave of John Miller. He asks his wife for reassurance, "Tell me I have led a good life… tell me I'm a good man." Motivated by gratitude, James Ryan wanted his life to honor John Miller.

Out of gratitude to Jesus for the proof that he has always loved us, loves us now, and will always love us, we are called to love others. This is not something we generate on our own effort, but rather something the Holy Spirit works in us, as the Apostle Paul wrote to the Galatians, "the fruit of the Spirit is love…" (5:22). Loving others is what Jesus calls us to do in response to his love for us.

The three-fold vision God is unfolding here at Christ Church is to preach the Gospel, love people, and trust God to change lives. The Gospel is that Jesus has always loved us, loves us now, and will always love us—and that he proved it in dying on the cross to atone for our sins. Loving people is what we are called to do in response. God the Holy Spirit changes our lives with God's love and enables us to love others in response.

So be encouraged. Jesus has always loved you, loves you now, and will always love you. Jesus loves you because God the Father loves Jesus ("As the Father has loved me, so I have loved you").

As Jesus repeated to his disciples at the Last Supper, "I have loved you... I have loved you." It's neither the repetitions of a TV character nor a silly love song. It's the Gospel.

Amen.

MERCY TRIUMPHS OVER JUDGMENT
Pageants, Pensions, and the Gospel Lens Cap

For judgment will be without mercy to anyone who has shown no mercy; mercy triumphs over judgment (James 2:13).

In the Name of the Father, Son, and Holy Spirit.

Back in the mid-90s my family and I lived in Wyoming, where I served in youth ministry. We attended the local high school graduation, joining a family with whom we'd become good friends. The parents were so excited to see their one and only child graduate from high school. They asked me to videotape the graduation for them so they could simply sit back and enjoy the commencement ceremony. I was honored by their request and arrived early and took the time to set up the camera at a great angle, etc. I videotaped the whole ceremony, sure that I had done a great job.

A couple evenings later we all gathered at their house to watch it. There was just one snag: while the audio was great, the screen was black. We could hear everything, but we couldn't see a thing. For all my efforts in trying to capture great camera angles and the like I had neglected to take the lens cap off. Needless to say, I felt so bad about this, but this family was really sweet—they laughed and hugged me and told me not to worry about it. Then for the next couple hours we watched the blank screen and listened to ceremony, taking turns trying to help one another visualize what we were "watching."

Today's reading from the Letter of James is a well-known passage about faith and works, and there has been much argument and discussion about the idea that faith without works is dead, the relationship between faith and works, that if we're saved by faith and not by works, what does it mean that faith without works is dead? But in the midst of these arguments and discussions we often miss the main point of the Gospel. We make sure our arguments address the faith-versus-works debate from all the right angles, but we forget to take the cap off the lens and are therefore blind to what stands at the root of this passage. The main point of the Gospel is not faith-versus-works, because faith and works has to do with our response to the Gospel, and the heart of the gospel is not what *we* do for God, but what God *has done* for us in Jesus Christ. The heart of the Gospel is these four words ... "*mercy triumphs over judgment*" (2:13).

Mercy triumphs over judgment.

Our culture is obsessed with judging others. Many of the most popular "reality" television shows are centered on judgment. One show, *Toddlers and Tiaras*, is about beauty pageants for toddlers. Little girls, three-, four-, five-years-old, primped and postured and pronounced by their appearance? But it's a booming business. (By the way, for any students trying to figure out what to major in, my guess is that along with the fast-growing industry of beauty pageants for toddlers there will be an equally fast-growing need for child psychiatrists.)

The most popular show on television, *American Idol*, is centered on what judges think about a contestant's singing ability. The heart of the show is not really the singing of the contestants, but the judge's commentaries. Randy may say something like, "Yo, yo, keeping it real, dog—you did your thing—you got *pipes!*—props to you, *dog!*" while Simon may say something like, "That was absolutely awful—I felt like I was watching a poor attempt at karaoke at a cheap hotel bar" and Paula may say something like, "I... I... I just... I just love you... you are a bright and shining star!" Of course, millions of Americans join in the judging and phone in their verdicts.

But being judged is not just a mainstay on television; it is an integral part of our culture, an integral part of human nature. Judging and being judged is a part of life from cradle to grave. We're judged by our circumstances, by the color of our skin, by our neighborhood, by our school—how we dress, who we marry, what we drive, where we *belong*, how smart or athletic our kids are, where *they* go to college, where we then retire... judging and being judged never stops.

And often we do things we regret in an attempt to *win* favorable judgment from others. We endure things that we should never feel compelled to endure in order to belong—of course there's hazing and rushing, but later there's buying vehicles and remodeling houses that we don't need or can't afford. It never stops.

Being judged often happens in churches—and we are faced with feeling judged and found wanting or becoming hypocrites who judge others. When I lived in South Carolina I was a youth minister at large church. As the youth ministry grew many kids from outside the church were showing up. Some of these kids were from other churches, hopping from one youth ministry to another with their friends, but many more were from outside the church altogether, and dressed and acted as such—and they were showing up because they felt welcomed and because God in his grace was doing good things in the ministry. One kid actually wore a bathrobe to the youth group gatherings—no joke—he had clothes on underneath, but instead of a light jacket or sweatshirt he enjoyed wearing a bathrobe—apparently he wanted to be like Christopher Walken. Anyway, one parent in the church took objection to this and asked me to meet him for lunch. He was a wonderful man, a respected leader in the community, always very kind to my family and me, but he had it out for robe boy. After the initial small talk, he tried to convince me to keep kids like robe boy out of the youth ministry because they would corrupt the other kids. (I'm not making this up). Naturally, I respectfully listened, but of course we couldn't keep kids like robe boy out of the youth ministry.

The Church is to be a place where people receive mercy, not judgment, because Scripture tells us that mercy triumphs over judgment.

This idea is not just found in the New Testament, but throughout the Old Testament as well. When Moses encountered God on Mt. Sinai, God revealed himself with these words, "The Lord, the Lord, a God *merciful* and gracious, slow to anger, and abounding in steadfast love and faithfulness" (Exodus 34:6). In Psalm 136 the phrase *"His mercy endures forever"* is found twenty-six times (*BCP*, 789-791). In the midst of the devastation following the razing of Jerusalem by the Babylonians Jeremiah wrote, "The steadfast love of the Lord never ceases, *his mercies never come to an end; they are new every morning"* (Lamentations 3:22). The latter Old Testament prophet, Micah spoke these words: "(God) has told you... what is good; and what does the Lord require of you but... *to love mercy* and to walk humbly with your God" (Micah 6:8).

At the Sermon of the Mount Jesus preached, *"Blessed are the merciful, for they will receive mercy"* (Matthew 5:7). Regarding how to treat other people Jesus preached, *"Be merciful, just as your Father is merciful"* (Luke 6:36), and He told the parable of the *unmerciful servant* (Matthew 18:23-35) to illustrate this.

The good news of the Gospel is that God gives us mercy in Jesus Christ, because God in Christ took upon Himself our due judgment. The Greek word "mercy" in the New Testament, *eleos,* is proactive and focuses on meeting the needs of the recipient whether or not the recipient has a claim on the giver. In other words, when it comes to the mercy of God, God is the one who proactively takes the initiative and gives us mercy in spite of the fact that we have no claim on it whatsoever. God gives us his mercy out of his grace.

This summer I read *Black Hawk Down*, Mark Bowden's gripping account of American Black Hawk helicopters being shot down in Mogadishu, Somalia in October 1993. One of the Army Rangers who was shot down was Mike Durant. After the crash he found himself alone with a broken leg, out of ammunition, out of options. At that point an angry mob discovered him. Bowden writes:

> Durant kept his eyes on the sky as the mob
> closed over him. They were screaming things
> he couldn't understand. When a man struck
> him in the face with a rifle butt it broke his
> nose and shattered the bone around his eye.
> People pulled at his arms and legs, and then
> others began tearing at his clothes... He gave
> himself over to them... His boots were
> yanked off, his survival vest, and his shirt. ..
> All the while he was being kicked and hit...
> Then someone threw a handful of dirt in his
> face, which went into his mouth. They tied a
> rag or towel over the top of his head and eyes,
> and the mob hoisted him up in the air, partly

carrying and partly dragging him... He was buffeted from all sides, kicked, hit with fists and rifle butts. He could not see where they were taking him. He was engulfed in a great wave of hate and anger (197).

Durant's captors considered him worth more alive than dead, and so he eventually survived.

In the same way Durant was "engulfed in a great wave of hate and anger," Jesus was engulfed by hateful and angry religious leaders and Roman soldiers. In the same way Durant "gave himself over" to his captors, Jesus gave himself over to receive the judgment for our sins. In the same way Durant was "hoisted up in the air" Jesus was hoisted up on a cross. Jesus, because of the mercy of God, took the judgment in our place.

Mercy triumphs over judgment.

I recently read Michael Lewis' bestselling book, *The Blind Side*, which recounts the incredible story of Michael Oher, a poor kid from the projects of Memphis who was cared for by a well-to-do Christian family and given a second chance at life. He ended up going to play football at Ole Miss and was eventually drafted in the first round by the Baltimore Ravens, where he plays left tackle and protects "the blind side" of the Ravens' quarterbacks. In this book Michael is very to-the-point when speaking of the family who cared for him: "I wasn't anything when I first got to them, and they loved me anyway... Nothing was in it for them" (p. 314).

In spite of our sin, God loves us anyway. Scripture tells us, "God proves his love for us in that while we were still sinners Christ died for us" (Romans 5:8). God did this because, as Paul wrote to the Ephesians, God is "rich in mercy" (2:4).

Mercy triumphs over judgment.

In our liturgy we are reminded of the mercy of God each week in the prayer of humble access, which we pray before receiving Holy Communion, as we acknowledge that we do not trust our own righteousness, but rather trust in God's *"manifold and great mercies,"* and we remember that God's *"property is always to have mercy" (The Book of Common Prayer, 337).*

The heart of the Gospel has never been about what you do, nor how much you've argued faith-versus-works. The heart of the Gospel is what God has done *for* you in Jesus Christ, who died for the sins of the world, who took your due judgment upon himself, who had *mercy* on you.

And why does God have mercy on you? Because he loves you.

I once visited a lady who was on her deathbed, surrounded by her husband and grown children, one of whom read a card that her granddaughter had made for her: Written in big words in crayon were these words: "Dear Grandma, Soon you will be going up, up, up, up, up. I love you, I love you, I love you, I love you, I love you. I love you because I love you."

God has mercy on you because he loves you.

From the cradle to the grave you may receive judgment from the world, but from the cradle to the grave you receive mercy from God. Perhaps today the Holy Spirit will take the lens cap off your hearts so that you can see the heart of the Gospel—mercy triumphs over judgment.

Amen.

GOD IS ON YOUR SIDE
Songs for the Road of Despair

*If the Lord had not been on our side, let Israel
now say;
if the Lord had not been on our side... (Psalm
124:1-2, BCP 781).*

In the Name of the Father, Son, and Holy Spirit.

I love road trips. I love getting in my truck with a cup of
coffee and music for the road, knowing that I have a long
drive in front of me. Choosing albums for the drive is one of
the best parts about getting ready for a road trip--some U2,
Neil Young, Elton John, some Brian Regan for laughs and
Mozart for sophistication. For me, no road trip is complete
without the proper tunes. One of my favorite movies,
Elizabethtown (2005 film with Orlando Bloom and Kirsten

Dunst) culminates with a classic road trip sequence, replete with a moving soundtrack.

Songs for the road are nothing new. Today I'm preaching from an ancient song for the road, Psalm 124. Psalm 124 is a "Psalm of Ascent" or "Gradual Psalm," one of the fifteen psalms (Psalms 120 through 134) that were recited or sung by the Israelites while walking to Jerusalem for one of the major annual feasts. Each year they would ascend the roads to Jerusalem in the early spring for the Feast of Passover, the early summer for the Feast of Pentecost, and the autumn for the Feast of Tabernacles. Psalms 120 through 134 were their songs for the road.

Psalm 124 is a beautiful song that reminds us of something we often forget: God is on your side.

It begins by reminding you twice that God is on your side: "If the Lord had not been on our side, let Israel now say; if the Lord had not been on our side…"

As you know, it's easier to believe God is on your side when things are going well in your life, when you're feeling blessed by God. But it doesn't stop there, because the good news is that God is on your side when things are not going well. God is on your side *especially* when things are not going well. As I heard preached once, "God's office is at the end of your rope."

The greatest difficulties in our lives can often be attributed to either people or circumstances. Psalm 124 mentions both:

> If the Lord had not been on our side, let Israel
> now say; If the Lord had not been on our side,
> when enemies rose up against us; Then would
> they have swallowed us up alive in their fierce
> anger toward us; Then would the waters have
> overwhelmed us and the torrent gone over us;

Then would the raging waters have gone
right over us.

Sometimes people in our lives—including ourselves—rise up
like enemies. And there are other times when we are
overwhelmed by circumstances that simply *happen*. As Psalm
124 demonstrates, there are times in our lives when we feel
swallowed up by other people, or by our own mistakes, times
in our lives when we feel like we're drowning—in sorrow or
sickness or despair or debt or any number of things. At times
we find ourselves utterly overwhelmed, in situations that are
bigger than us, situations in which only God can help.

Psalm 124 meets us along that road and reminds us that
when we are dealing with difficulties brought about by
people or ourselves or circumstances, God is on our side.

Eugene Petersen, best known for his translation of the Bible
entitled *The Message*, wrote a book on the Gradual Psalms
entitled, *A Long Obedience in the Same Direction*, which
includes a helpful chapter on Psalm 124. Listen to what he
says about Psalm 124:

> Good poetry survives not when it is pretty or
> beautiful or nice but when it is true: accurate
> and honest. The psalms are great poetry and
> have lasted not because they appeal to our
> fantasies and our wishes but because they are
> confirmed in the intensities of honest and
> hazardous living. Psalm 124 is not a selected
> witness, inserted like a commercial into our
> lives to testify that life goes better with God;
> it is not part of a media blitz to convince us
> that God is superior to all the other gods on
> the market. It is not a press release. It is an
> honest prayer (75).

Christians, like everyone else, often deal with suffering. It's
always been that way. The early Church was no stranger to

suffering. Paul's Letter to the Romans was written to Christians who were undergoing persecution at the hand of the Romans, for at that time Christianity was neither recognized nor tolerated in the Roman Empire. When Paul wrote his Letter to the Romans the Roman Emperor was Nero, who ruled from 54-68 A.D. The notorious Nero killed his mother, killed his wife, killed his stepfather, and killed his unborn child to keep his power—and he didn't stop there. After the great fire of Rome in July of 64, Nero fixed the blame on Christians and set about on a massive persecution, killing many. The famous Roman historian, Tacitus describes the deaths of Christian under Nero:

> Mockery of every sort was added to their deaths. Covered with the skins of beasts, they were torn by dogs and perished, or were nailed to crosses, or were doomed to the flames and burnt, to serve as a nightly illumination, when daylight had expired (Tacitus, *Annals* XV, 44).

And yet, as Paul wrote in his Letter to the Romans, in spite of their suffering, God was still on the side of the Christians. Listen to what Paul wrote to the Christians in Rome suffering persecution under Nero:

> If God is for us, who is against us? He who did not withhold his own Son, but gave him up for all of us, will he not with him also give us everything else?... Who will separate us from the love of Christ? Will hardship, or distress, or persecution, or famine, or nakedness, or peril, or sword? ... No, in all these things we are more than conquerors through him who loved us. For I am convinced that neither death, nor life, nor angels, nor rulers, nor things present, nor things to come, nor powers, nor height, nor depth, nor anything else in all creation, will

be able to separate us from the love of God in Christ Jesus our Lord (Romans 8:31b-32, 35, 37-39).

In fact, Paul was himself eventually beheaded—and he emphasizes that not even death can separate you from the love of God in Christ, because God is on your side.

It is when things are hardest in our lives that we need to know God is standing by us, that God is on our side. Often our lives are not so much a long obedience in the same direction, but a long *dis*obedience in the same direction. And yet that doesn't stop the love of God. God *still* stands by your side.

In 1961 Ben E. King wrote the classic song, "Stand by Me," for the doo wop group, The Drifters, but The Drifters passed on it and so Ben recorded it himself. You may know these lyrics by heart:

> When the night has come
> And the land is dark
> And the moon is the only light we'll see
> No I won't be afraid, no I won't be afraid
> Just as long as you stand, stand by me
> If the sky that we look upon
> Should tumble and fall
> And the mountains should crumble to the sea
> I won't cry, I won't cry, no I won't shed a tear
> Just as long as you stand, stand by me

"Stand by Me" expresses the longing that we all have to not be alone, especially when times are hard, the longing that we all have for someone to stand by us, to be on our side.

If we fast-forward about thirty-three years after "Stand by Me" was released, we hear another song along these lines, the 1994 hit by The Pretenders, "I'll Stand By You." This song answers the longing expressed in Ben E. King's "Stand by Me," as Chrissie Hynde sings:

> When the night falls on you, you don't know what to do
> Nothing you confess could make me love you less
> I'll stand by you

The Gospel is in this song, because God in Jesus Christ has shown all of us that he stands by us. Nothing you confess could make him love you less.

In Psalm 124 we see that not only is God on our side, ultimately he will deliver us from all the hard times in our lives, those caused by people, including ourselves, and those caused by circumstances that we didn't see coming. As Psalm 124:6 says: "Blessed be the Lord! He has not given us over to be a prey for their teeth."

Indeed, God "has not given us over to be a prey," because God the Son, Jesus Christ, was "given over" for us. Each year Jesus walked the roads up to Jerusalem for the annual feasts, and surely recited or sang the Psalms of Ascents, including Psalm 124, as he did so. In the second chapter of the Gospel According to Luke we read of the twelve-year old Jesus walking to Jerusalem with his family for Passover. A little over twenty years later Jesus walked these same roads with his disciples to celebrate the Passover. It's likely that again he recited or sang these Psalms, including Psalm 124, as he did so.

And after the Last Supper, Jesus willingly gave himself over in our place. As Paul wrote to the Galatians, Jesus "gave himself for our sins to set us free (1:4):" and as he wrote to Titus, Jesus "gave himself for us that he might redeem us from all iniquity" (2:14).

This summer my wife and I watched the film, *Taken*, in which Liam Neeson stars as a retired CIA operative who rescues his teenage daughter who has been abducted in Paris and kept to be sold on the black market as a bride for the highest bidder. One of the most moving parts of the film is when Liam Neeson is on cell phone with his daughter, who is hiding under the bed trying to elude the kidnappers in the apartment. He tells her she will be taken, and asks her to leave her cell phone on so he can hear it happen and try to gain some clues. Neeson listens from across the Atlantic as his daughter is abducted by the kidnappers, who find her under the bed—it's a heartbreaking scene. Fortunately, of course, he rescues her in the end.

God "has not given us over to be a prey," because Jesus Christ gave himself over in our place—and God the Father watched and listened as Jesus Christ was given over on our behalf, taken by the Roman authorities—mocked, beaten, humiliated, and nailed to a cross. And because Jesus was given over in our place, as Psalm 124 reminds us not once but twice, "we have escaped:" "*We have escaped* like a bird from the snare of the fowler; the snare is broken and *we have escaped.*"

Jesus gave himself over to death on the cross because God is on our side, and because God is on our side even death is not the end of the story. Psalm 124 tells us, "If the Lord had not been on our side... (our enemies) "would... have swallowed us up alive." But God is on our side, and as Paul wrote to the Corinthians, even death, the last and greatest enemy is swallowed up in victory: "Death has been *swallowed up* in victory... thanks be to God, who gives us the victory through our Lord, Jesus Christ" (1 Cor. 15:54b and 57).

Finally, Psalm 124 ends by reminding us once again that God is on our side: "Our help is in the Name of the Lord, the maker of heaven and earth."

And that is the good news of the Gospel. The One who created you, "the Maker of heaven and earth," is on your side.

God is more powerful than your enemies—even if that enemy is *you*—God is on your side.

God is more powerful than the biggest and most confusing difficulties in your life, and in his time he will deliver you. You will not be given over because Jesus was given over in your place. God is on your side now. He stands by you. Nothing you confess will make him love you less. Nothing, not even death, can separate you from the love of God, because God is on your side.

So perhaps on your next road trip you'll remember Psalm 124, an ancient track that reminds us that God is on your side.

Amen.

HIS GRACE IS ENOUGH
Bad Teachers, Chalkboards, and the Only Lesson that Matters

He is the reflection of God's glory and the exact imprint of God's very being, and he sustains* all things by his powerful word. When he had made purification for sins, he sat down at the right hand of the Majesty on high (Hebrews 1:3).

In the Name of the Father, Son, and Holy Spirit.

Take a moment and try to remember your all time favorite school teacher—maybe a teacher from elementary, middle or high school, maybe a university professor—the teacher whose class you looked forward to, the teacher who taught with kindness. Then take a moment and think of your least favorite teacher, the one whose class caused fits of anxiety, the one whose class you could not wait to finish.

When I was in first grade my family moved mid-school year. I found myself in a big school, the new kid in class, very awkward and uncomfortable. During my first day there we had "quiet time" during which we were supposed to read or color silently. I committed the cardinal sin of whispering a question to the girl sitting next to me, "Can I borrow a red crayon?" There was a collective gasp on the part of the kids, and then the teacher ripped into me. Unlike the crayon I asked for, *I* turned *purple* with shame and ended up staying in during my first recess to write on the chalkboard the following sentence: "I will never talk during quiet time again." I had to write it thirty times. I couldn't even tell you that teacher's name, but from my first day of class I received no grace from her. On the last day of school I remember sprinting out of that classroom as though I had been set free.

Fast-forward five years to sixth grade. That first day I walked into class with sweaty palms, classically apprehensive about what the teacher would be like and which kids would be in my class. The teacher, Mrs. Cole, whom I had never met, walked over to me, wearing her Coke-bottle glasses and yellow sweater, and gave me a hug. "I'm so glad you're in my class," she grinned, "We're going to have a great school year." And we did. Mrs. Cole was awesome. She smiled a lot, took the time to get to know each of us in the class, read us J.R.R. Tolkien books, and laughed with us each day. I learned so much that year. The kids with other teachers were jealous, "You're in Mrs. Cole's class? Lucky...." Mrs. Cole gave all of us in her class the great gift of grace. From the moment we walked into her class on the first day of school she assured us that we had her favor, that we would be treated with grace, and that allowed us to have a great school year.

As far as classroom management goes, God is not like my first grade teacher, waiting for us to mess up so we can be punished and repeat promises that we can't keep. God is more like Mrs. Cole, giving us grace and favor from the very first moment of the very first day of school.

God's grace is enough.

This past Thursday night I had the privilege of joining about 60,000 of my fan-friends at Scott Stadium for the U2 concert. They've been one of my favorite bands from middle school to middle age, and the concert was no disappointment. One recurring theme in U2's lyrics is this theme of grace. The last track of their classic 2001 album, *All That You Can't Leave Behind*, is entitled, "Grace," and begins:

> Grace—she takes the blame
> She covers the shame
> Removes the stain
> It could be her name
> Grace—it's a name for a girl
> It's also a thought that changed the world

The song, "Breathe," on their latest album, *No Line on the Horizon*, is another example: "I found grace, it's all that I found, and I can breathe, breathe now."

We preach a lot about grace here at Christ Church because, as the Apostle Paul wrote to the Ephesians, "By *grace* you have been saved through faith, and this is not your own doing; it is the gift of God" (2:8).

The ultimate source of the grace of God is found in Jesus Christ, as John wrote in the prologue of his account of the Gospel: "From his fullness we have all received grace upon grace… grace and truth came through Jesus Christ" (1:16-17). Grace is indeed "a thought that changed the world," and because we have found grace in Jesus Christ, we "can breathe now."

In Paul Zahl's powerful book, *Grace in Practice*, he defines grace this way:

> Grace is love that seeks you out when you
> have nothing to give in return. Grace is love

coming at you that has nothing to do with you. Grace is being loved when you are unlovable. It is being loved when you are the opposite of lovable. The cliché definition of grace is unconditional love. It is a true cliché... Grace is a love that has nothing to do with you, the beloved. It has everything and only to do with the lover... Grace is one-way love (36).

From the very beginning God has given us his grace, his one-way love in Jesus Christ.

Today's scripture is from the Letter to the Hebrews, which was written to Christians who had converted from Judaism to Christianity and were suffering persecution under Roman rule. At that time Judaism was recognized by the Romans, but Christianity was not, so due to the persecution many of the Jewish converts to Christianity were returning to the safety of Judaism. The Letter to the Hebrews was written to demonstrate that Jesus Christ, the Son of God, had fulfilled in his death on the cross all the legal and ceremonial requirements of Judaism. In other words, God's grace in Christ is enough.

In today's passage the writer tells us that "God has spoken to us by a Son... through whom he also created the worlds" (Hebrews 1:2). God gave us his grace in Jesus Christ even before we were born. When God created us in his image, he did so through Jesus Christ. We also see this in the Gospel According to John—"All things came into being through him (Jesus Christ), and without him not one thing came into being" (1:3) and in Paul's Letter to the Colossians—"in him (Jesus Christ) all things in heaven and on earth were created... all things have been created through him and for him" (1:15-16).

God gave us his grace in Jesus Christ even before we were born—just as God told the prophet Jeremiah: "Before I formed you in the womb, I knew you, and before you were born I consecrated you" (Jeremiah 1:5).

Many people feel like God made a mistake when he created them, or that maybe they are simply a chemical accident with no purpose. But no one is a mistake. God created all of us in his image and has given us his grace, his one-way love in Jesus Christ.

There is an idea out there that when it comes to the Trinity, God the Father is the mean Person, Jesus is the nice Person, and the Holy Spirit is the Person along for the ride. But Scripture is clear that all three Persons of the Trinity give us grace.

In fact, if we want to know what God the Father is like, we look to Jesus. In today's passage we see that Jesus "is the reflection of God's glory and the *exact imprint* of God's very being" (1:3). So not only does grace come to us in Jesus Christ, it comes to us from God the Father because Jesus is "the exact imprint of God's very being." And we read in Paul's Letters to the Romans (8:15-17) and Galatians (4:6) that the Holy Spirit is the one who allows us to experience the grace of God, that indeed God is our Heavenly Father and we are his children.

The ultimate expression of the grace of God is the death of Jesus Christ on the cross for the sins of the world. In fact, in today's passage the writer, after describing Jesus Christ as the Son of God and the creator of all things, immediately points to the cross: "When he (Jesus Christ) had made purification for sins, he sat down at the right hand of the Majesty on high" (1:3).

Notice that Jesus' purification for sins has already been completed, period, full stop: "when he *had made* purification for sins." Jesus' death on the cross for the sins of the world is the primary demonstration of the grace God gives us. Our sins have been atoned for, once for all, totally and completely.

After Jesus' death, resurrection and ascension he was seated at the right hand of God, his mission of making "purification for sins" finished. This is a main theme in the Letter to the Hebrews, as we see not only in today's passage. In chapter eight, we are told "we have such a high priest, one who is seated at the right hand of the throne of the Majesty in the heavens" (8:1); in chapter ten, that "when Christ had offered for all time a single sacrifice for sins, he sat down at the right hand of God" (10:12); and in chapter twelve, that Jesus Christ "endured the cross, disregarding its shame, and has taken his seat at the right hand of the throne of God" (12:2).

Jesus died on the cross for our sins because of his grace, his one-way love for us. In the latter part of today's passage the writer makes this crystal clear: (Jesus Christ) is "now crowned with glory and honor because of the suffering of death, so that by the grace of God he might taste death for everyone" (2:9).

God's grace is enough.

As for U2's grace-focus, I recently read Steven Stockman's fascinating book, *Walk On: The Spiritual Journey of U2*, and he powerfully describes the fact that it takes awhile for the grace of God to seep into our hearts:

> There is something about grace that makes even those who believe in it find it hard to believe in. You can hear the words and take hold of the understanding that here is an upside-down world order where the first are last and the last are first and where acceptance is unmerited. In a world where the first are first and the only way to be affirmed is to be the most intelligent or best-looking or most successful, it is hard to get

reconditioned to the conditioning of grace. A flower doesn't bloom in one hour of sunlight, and a believer's soul needs constant exposure to the rays of grace day after day, year after year, before it moves from an intellectual assent to a truth that our lives bask in and live by (161-162).

It often takes a long time for the reality of God's grace to seep into our hearts. God knows that, and one of the ways he reminds us of his grace is through the sacrament of Holy Communion. Listen to how Thomas Cranmer, one of my heroes and the leading figure in the English Reformation, describes how God reminds us of his grace at Holy Communion:

Sacraments ordained of Christ... (are) effectual signs of grace, and God's good will towards us, by the which he doth work invisibly in us, and doth not only quicken, but also strengthen and confirm our Faith in him (BCP, 872).

So we see in today's passage from Hebrews that God has given us his grace, his one-way love in Jesus Christ from before we were born, and that the ultimate demonstration of that grace is in the death of Jesus Christ on the cross in which he "made purification for sins" once and for all and was seated at the right hand of God the Father. Because of the grace of God, Jesus tasted death for everyone.

God knows it takes a long time for the reality of his grace to seep into our hearts, and he has given us the sacrament of Holy Communion as an "effectual sign of grace" to help that happen.

There's no need to stress about how this Teacher is going to treat you, because what U2 sings is true: grace "takes the blame," "covers the shame," and "removes the stain;" and because of God's grace in Jesus Christ, we can "breathe now."

God's grace is enough.

Amen.

GETTING OVER YOURSELF
The Baptismal Death to Self-Reliance

James and John, the sons of Zebedee, came forward to him and said to him, "Teacher, we want you to do for us whatever we ask of you." And he said to them, "What is it you want me to do for you?" And they said to him, "Grant us to sit, one at your right hand and one at your left, in your glory." But Jesus said to them, "You do not know what you are asking" (Mark 10:35-38a).

In the Name of the Father, Son, and Holy Spirit.

A couple years ago I read a book by John Maxwell called *Failing Forward*, which is about moving forward when things in our lives do not go as we planned, which eventually happens to all of us. My favorite chapter in this book is called, "Get Over Yourself—Everyone Else Has," which describes the dangers of being self-absorbed and self-centered—the dangers of what we call narcissism.

The word "narcissism" comes from a character in Greek mythology named Narcissus, who was famous for his good looks, but who treated others with cruelty. Narcissus became so infatuated with his own reflection in a pool of water that he could not stop admiring it and ended up dying there. Narcissism leads to death.

Narcissism, being self-absorbed and self-centered, is native to all of us. We want what we want when we want it. We look out for number one. We are the center of our own little universe. Perhaps you've seen the hilarious offbeat 2001 film, *Zoolander*, in which Ben Stiller, who plays male model, Derek Zoolander, asks the profound question, "Have you ever wondered if there was more to life, other than being really, really, ridiculously good looking?" Derek Zoolander, like you and me, has some issues with narcissism.

Extreme narcissism is known as "Narcissistic Personality Disorder." Listen to how the Mayo Clinic describes this:

> Narcissistic Personality Disorder is a mental disorder in which people have an inflated sense of their own importance and a deep need for admiration. They believe that they're superior to others and have little regard for other people's feelings. But behind this mask of ultra-confidence lies a fragile self-esteem, vulnerable to the slightest criticism... Narcissistic personality disorder crosses the border of healthy confidence and self-esteem into thinking so highly of yourself that you put yourself on a pedestal.
>
> Symptoms of Narcissistic Personality Disorder include the following: believing that you're better than others, exaggerating your

achievements or talents, expecting constant praise and admiration, failing to recognize other people's emotions and feelings, taking advantage of others, expressing disdain for those you feel are inferior, being jealous of others and believing that others are jealous of you, trouble keeping healthy relationships, setting unrealistic goals, and appearing as tough-minded or unemotional.

Narcissism does a lot of damage. It can shatter personal lives, torpedo relationships and marriages, estrange parents and children, and wreak havoc in churches. Narcissism can take down companies, split great rock 'n roll bands, and keep talented sports teams from winning. The narcissism of others has caused damage in my life, and my own narcissism has caused damage in others' lives. I suspect it's the same with you.

Narcissism is found in all of us because at the heart of narcissism is original sin. Scripture tells us that we are all self-absorbed and self-centered. In the book of Isaiah we see that "All we like sheep have gone astray; we have all turned to our own way" (53:6a) and in the New Testament we see in Paul's Letter to the Romans that "all have sinned and fall short of the glory of God" (3:23).

Even Jesus' own disciples were prone to narcissism. You would think that after spending about three years with the Son of God that you would get over yourself a little bit, but apparently not. In the Gospel According to Mark Jesus predicts his death and resurrection three times to his disciples (8:31; 9:30-32; and 10:32-34). In Jesus' third prediction of his death and resurrection Jesus pulls the twelve aside and tells them:

> The Son of Man will be handed over to the chief priests and the scribes, and they will condemn him to death; then they will hand

him over to the Gentiles; they will mock him, and spit upon him, and flog him, and kill him; and after three days he will rise again (10:33-34).

And how did the disciples respond to Jesus' prediction of his death and resurrection? With narcissism. That's where today's Gospel lesson picks up. Listen to what James and John do: "James and John, the sons of Zebedee, came forward to him (Jesus) and said to him, 'Teacher, we want you to do for us whatever we ask of you.'"

It wasn't just any two of the disciples who told Jesus this; it was James and John. Along with Peter, James and John were considered the "inner three" disciples. They were the three disciples who were with Jesus when he raised Jairus' daughter from the dead and when he was transfigured on the mountain and appeared with Moses and Elijah. They were the three who later would be with Jesus in the Garden of Gethsemane immediately before Jesus was betrayed. Jesus had just told them for the third time about his impending suffering, death, and resurrection, and they respond by saying, "Teacher, we want you to do for us whatever we ask of you."

Jesus is gracious in his response, "What is it you want me to do for you?"

James and John respond, "Grant us to sit, one at your right hand and one at your left, in your glory." Their response to Jesus' prediction of his impending death and resurrection was a request for power, dripping with narcissism. Jesus responds by letting James and John know that they are clueless, "You do not know what you are asking." Then he asks them a question: "Are you able to drink the cup that I drink, or be baptized with the baptism that I am baptized with?" In their hubris James and John reply, "We are able."

And yet, isn't that what happens in our own lives? When it comes to the Christian faith, don't we often wonder, "What's in it for me?" Don't we often respond to things about which we are clueless with hubris and self-reliance? We *know* we can handle it. We've got it *covered.* "We are able."

Jesus does two things in response to James and John. First, he assures them that indeed they will drink the cup he will drink, and they will be baptized with the baptism with which he will be baptized.

In the Old Testament "cup" is a metaphor for drinking the wrath of God, as we see in Psalm 75:8—"For in the Lord's hand is a cup, full of spiced and foaming wine, which he pours out, and all the wicked of the earth shall drink and drain the dregs" (*The Book of Common Prayer* 691; see also Isaiah 51:17-23 and Jeremiah 49:12).

Similarly, in the Old Testament "baptism" is a metaphor for being overwhelmed by sorrow and grief, as we see in Psalm 69:16—"Save me from the mire; do not let me sink; let me be rescued from those who hate me and out of the deep waters" (*The Book of Common Prayer* 680; see also Psalm 124:4-5 and Isaiah 43:2). In other words, James and John would share the suffering of Jesus. This came to pass, as James was later executed with a sword by order of King Herod (Acts 12:2) and John was exiled as an old man to the island of Patmos (Revelation 1:9).

Second, Jesus lets James and John know that it was not his decision as to whether or not they would be granted to sit with him in glory: "To sit at my right hand or at my left is not mine to grant, but it is for those for whom it has been prepared."

How did the other disciples respond to the narcissism of James and John? They got fired up, as Mark writes with some understatement, "When the ten heard this, they began to be angry with James and John." Peter, the third of the inner three, was probably especially angry. We are all familiar with the fun and games of rivalry, ambition, and jockeying for position. It is part of our lives from the sibling rivalry of childhood, throughout our years in school, and often throughout our careers and even into our later years. Narcissism is no respecter of age. And as was the case with the disciples, narcissism often leads to resentment and anger.

Jesus then calls all the disciples together and cuts to the chase when it comes to narcissism: "Whoever wishes to become great among you must be your servant, and whoever wishes to be first among you must be slave of all." In other words, the antidote to narcissism is service.

Dr. Karl Menninger, a famous psychiatrist, was once asked, "What would you advise a person to do if he felt a nervous breakdown coming on?" Menninger replied, "Find someone in need, and do something to help that person... generous people are rarely mentally ill people" (*Failing Forward* 102-103). The antidote to narcissism is service. And yet, we can even become prideful about how much we help others. While helping others and being generous can take the edge off of our narcissism a little bit, it does not address the root of our narcissism, original sin.

Thankfully, Jesus doesn't stop there. After telling his disciples, "whoever wishes to be first among you must be slave of all," Jesus points to the cross: "For the Son of Man came not to be served but to serve, and to give his life a ransom for many."

The phrase, "the Son of Man," is used often in reference to Jesus in the Gospel According to Mark. Jesus is also referred to as "the Son of God" by Mark, who begins his account of the Gospel with the words, "The beginning of the good news of Jesus Christ, the Son of God" (1:1). Jesus Christ is both the fully human "Son of Man," and the fully divine "Son of God."

And Jesus Christ, the "Son of Man" and "Son of God," took the form of a servant and gave his life as a ransom for the world, as Paul wrote to the Philippians, "Christ Jesus, who, those he was in the form of God, did not regard equality with God as something to be exploited, but emptied himself, taking the form of a slave... and became obedient to the point of death—even death on a cross" (2:6-8).

In his death on the cross Jesus did for us what we cannot do for ourselves, because when it comes to overcoming our narcissism, we are *not* able. We may believe, like James and John, "We are able," but we're not. As we saw earlier in Isaiah 53, indeed, "All we like sheep have gone astray" and "we have turned to our own way." And yet in Jesus' death, "the Lord has laid on him (Jesus) the iniquity of us all" (53:6b). And as we saw earlier in Romans 3, indeed, "all have sinned and fall short of the glory of God." And yet in Jesus' death we "are now justified by his grace as a gift, through the redemption that is in Christ Jesus" (3:24).

In fact, the word, "redemption," in Romans 3 and the word, "ransom," in Mark 10 refer to the same thing, the price being paid to set us free from all our sin, including our narcissism. In Jesus' day a ransom was paid to set free three kinds of people: slaves, prisoners of war, and those condemned to death. Because of the ransom Jesus paid in his death on the cross, we are no longer slaves to sin (including narcissism), we are no longer held captive as prisoners to the flesh, and we are no longer doomed to death.

Jesus has paid the ransom. We have been redeemed. We have been set free.

Even though Jesus prayed in the Garden of Gethsemane, "Father... remove this cup from me," he also prayed, "yet not what I want, but what you want" (Mark 14:36), and in his death on the cross Jesus drank the cup of judgment in our place. Moreover, in his death on the cross Jesus was baptized, overwhelmed and flooded, in suffering and grief in our place.

And in a similar way in which Jesus told James and John, "You do not know what you are asking," Jesus prayed for all of us, "Father, forgive them, for they do not know what they are doing" (Luke 23:34).

Jesus did these things for us because he loves us, because he gives us grace.

And Jesus did not stop there, because he also instituted two sacraments, Holy Baptism and Holy Communion, as signs of his grace. Jesus was baptized with suffering and grief so that we could be baptized into new life in him. Jesus drank the cup of judgment so that we could drink the cup of salvation.

So while there is some truth in the humorous saying, "Get over yourself—everyone else has," the deeper truth is that God has never gotten over you. We know this because Jesus took the form of a servant and gave his life on the cross as a ransom for you. He redeemed you with his blood. His death is the antidote for the narcissism of every person in the entire world, including James and John, including you and me. And Jesus now sits enthroned in glory at the right hand of God the Father, because that place of glory was prepared for him.

Amen.

THE WINE OF GRACE
The Only Way Out for a Dead Batmobile

On the third day there was a wedding in Cana of Galilee, and the mother of Jesus was there. Jesus and his disciples had also been invited to the wedding. When the wine gave out, the mother of Jesus said to him, "They have no wine." And Jesus said to her, "Woman, what concern is that to you and to me? My hour has not yet come." His mother said to the servants, "Do whatever he tells you." Now standing there were six stone water-jars for the Jewish rites of purification, each holding twenty or thirty gallons. Jesus said to them, "Fill the jars with water." And they filled them up to the brim. He said to them, "Now draw some out, and take it to the chief steward." So they took it. When the steward tasted the water that had become wine, and did not know where it came from (though the servants who had drawn the water knew), the steward called the bridegroom and said to him, "Everyone serves the good wine first, and then the inferior wine after the guests have become drunk. But you have kept the good wine until now." Jesus did this, the first of his signs, in Cana of Galilee, and revealed his glory; and his disciples believed in him (John 2:1-11).

In the Name of the Father, Son, and Holy Spirit.

Today I'm preaching on the Gospel passage about Jesus' first public miracle, when he changed water into wine at a wedding in Cana of Galilee. Cana was a very small village, and so the wedding was no doubt a community-wide event. Everyone of note in Cana was there, as were friends and family from neighboring villages, like Nazareth, so Jesus, his mother Mary, and some of his disciples were at the wedding. It was going well, everyone having a great time—some were even doing the "Electric Slide"—and then things come to a screeching halt because the booze runs out.

In Jesus' day running out of wine at a wedding reception was not a mild *faux pas*, it was considered extremely rude to the guests who had attended the wedding bearing gifts for the new couple. In fact, it was more than rude; it was offensive, so much so that there are actual records from Jesus' day of families being sued for running out of wine at a wedding. The wedding families found themselves facing an embarrassing and potentially threatening situation both socially and legally because "the wine gave out" (John 2:3).

Mary turns to Jesus when the wine gives out. "They have no wine," she tells him.

And that's often when we turn to God, isn't it? We turn to God when we run out of something—strength, money, options. We turn to God when lose passion or patience, we turn to God when we run out of hope or run out of joy. We turn to God when we're feeling beat-up and burned out. We turn to God when the game is up, when we might be found out, when we can no longer deny that we need help. We turn to God when we run out of something.

The good news of the Gospel is that God meets us where we have run out, that God meets us in that precise place of need.

That's what Jesus does at the wedding, even though at first it doesn't look that way. When Mary tells him the wine has run out, Jesus initially replies, "Woman, what concern is that to you and to me? My hour has not yet come." At first it appears that Jesus is out of line. After all, what would happen if you addressed your mother as "woman"? And yet, in Jesus' day, this expression was one of affection.

It's not that Jesus didn't care about the wine running out; it's that he knew he had come for a different purpose, he knew his "hour" had not come yet—again, we'll look at that later.

We know Jesus cares about the wine running out because he does *not* say, "Good. I'm glad the wine ran out. You shouldn't ever drink wine anyway, because wine is evil." He doesn't reprove the wedding families for not planning properly, he doesn't chastise the people for binge drinking, but he indeed does *something*. In fact, Mary *knows* he will do something because, in spite of Jesus' initial response, she tells the servants, "Do whatever he tells you."

Jesus sees six huge "stone water jars for the Jewish rites of purification." The Jews in Jesus' day had elaborate cleansing rituals in order to feel like they had purified themselves before eating, etc. Each of these jars held twenty to thirty gallons of water. Jesus says to the servants, "Fill the jars with water." They must have listened to Mary because "they filled them up to the brim."

Then Jesus told the servants to take some to the chief steward, so they did, and the chief steward tasted "the water that had become wine"—and not cheap wine, but the best wine. Instead of the bridegroom being chided for running out of wine and living with the stress and embarrassment of a matrimonial disaster, he is complimented for saving the best wine for last. Jesus changed the water into the best wine you could imagine. Why? Because Jesus cares about the details in your life, including running out of wine at a wedding.

Jesus tells us he knows even the number of hairs on our heads (Matthew 10:30). If you think about your life for a moment, what are the cares, preoccupations, and concerns enclosing you right now? What are the things in your life that you care about that even those closest to you might not know about? God knows them and God cares about them, precisely because he cares about you.

But there's much more to Jesus' miracle of changing water to wine. John writes, "Jesus did this, the first of his signs, in Cana of Galilee, and *revealed his glory.*" John only records seven such signs in his account of the Gospel. Those seven are for John the important *signs* of God *revealing his glory* in Jesus, as demonstrations that Jesus is more than just a great teacher or prophet, but that he is indeed the Son of God, the Messiah. In the prologue of John's Gospel we see this: "And the Word (Jesus) became flesh and lived among us, and *we have seen his glory,* the glory as of a father's only son, full of grace and truth" (1:14). When Jesus' changes the water into wine he is revealing to people the glory of God.

Revealing his glory is revealing his grace. Remember what the huge stone water jars were for? They were vessels for the water needed for ritual cleansing—six huge stone jars, each holding twenty to thirty gallons of water—gallons and gallons of water for the sake of people trying to make themselves clean before God according to law. Jesus fills these same huge stone jars with wine, the best wine you could imagine, as a free gift to people who had found themselves in a situation in which they had run out.

Here Jesus has changed the water of the law into the wine of grace. This also reflects these words of John from his prologue: "The law indeed was given through Moses; grace and truth came through Jesus Christ" (1:17).

It seems that the wine of grace is lost on most people's perspective on church. I can't tell you how many conversations I've had over the years with people outside of church who, when they find out that I'm clergy (which sometimes immediately kills the conversation), make a comment like, "Yeah, I really should get back to church, but there are things in my life I need to fix first;"or "I haven't been to church in so long... I'm sure God's not very impressed with me;" or "I'm not exactly the kind of person you want at church." At times I would guess you and I may share these same sentiments. And yet it is exactly people like us who *are* welcomed by Jesus, who came to seek and to save the lost, to restore the broken, to give his life in order to bring us back to God.

Our lives may be filled to the brim with our own rituals or laws or ways of trying to get our act together so we might be right with God, or with ourselves, but it never works in the long run. When we are in a situation in which *we* have run out, more rituals and practices aren't going to help; we need the grace of God. We don't need the water of the law; we need the wine of grace.

When I was young I received a toy Batmobile as a gift. It was so cool. When you pressed it on it would just automatically go and if it hit something, like a piece of furniture, it would reverse and then go forward again in a new direction. This would continue until one of two things happened: either it was turned off or the battery ran out of power. Until then, it would go, hit something, reverse, and go again in a new direction—over and over and over.

That's often what happens in our lives. We try to move forward until we hit a wall, then we back up, change directions and move forward again until we hit another wall—over and over and over. This happens in careers and in marriages, with besetting sins and compulsions. But eventually something happens and we get turned off or our internal battery runs out. Forward progress is lost on us and, in that place, the last thing we need is a new law. In that place we need the grace of God.

I recently read Gerhard Forde's powerful book, *On Being a Theologian of the Cross*, a helpful treatment of Martin Luther's Heidelberg Disputation of 1518. Forde describes how God meets us in that place of stalled progress:

> God is not... one who waits to approve those who have improved themselves, made themselves acceptable, or merited approval, but one who bestows good on the bad and needy... the love of God creates precisely out of nothing. Therefore the sinner must be reduced to nothing in order to be saved... Only the friends of the cross who have been reduced to nothing are properly prepared to receive the justifying grace poured out by the creative love of God. All other roads are closed (113-115).

There is one road open at the dead end, Jesus Christ, the way, the truth, and the life (John 14:6).

Jesus' water-to-wine miracle is a *sign*. Signs speak for themselves, but signs also point to something even more significant. There is something more significant to Jesus' response to his mother: "Woman, what concern is that to you and to me? My hour has not yet come."

Later Jesus' hour *did* come. After his triumphal entry into Jerusalem on Palm Sunday, Jesus told his disciples, *"The hour has come* for the Son of Man to be glorified" (12:23) and on the eve of his passion and death on the cross Jesus prayed, "Father, *the hour has come*; glorify your Son so that the Son may glorify You" (17:1).

When Jesus changes the water to wine he points ahead to his glory; on the cross, when his hour had come, carrying upon him the sins of the world, Jesus Christ revealed the glory of God in full.

And when Jesus revealed his glory by changing the water into wine, how did his disciples respond? John puts it very simply, *"His disciples believed in him."* Belief in Jesus as the Son of God and Savior of the world is a major theme in the Gospel According to John. In the first chapter John writes, "to all who received him, who *believed* in his name, he gave power to become children of God" (1:12) and near the end of his Gospel account he states that the gospel was written "so that you may come to *believe* that Jesus is the Messiah, the Son of God, and that through *believing* you may have life in his name" (20:31).

So what about you today?

Perhaps somewhere in your life you've just run out. Perhaps your internal battery is dead and you simply cannot move forward on your own anymore.

This miracle is about much more than water and wine—it is a sign that points us to the cross, where Jesus died to bring our helplessness under the law into the freedom of grace; to change despair to hope, sinners to saints, death to life. It is a story of resurrection. The first four words tell us this miracle took place "on the third day" (2:1), and Jesus was raised, when the hour had come, "on the third day."

And *your* hour has also come. God wants to fill you to the brim with the wine of his grace.

Amen.

HAVE MERCY ON ME, O GOD
Lenten Disciplines, Confession, and the Cry for Help

Have mercy on me, O God, according to your loving-kindness; in your great compassion blot out my offenses. Wash me through and through from my wickedness and cleanse me from my sin (Psalm 51:1-2, BCP 656).

In the Name of the Father, Son, and Holy Spirit.

Each year during the Ash Wednesday service we kneel and recite Psalm 51, one of the seven "Penitential Psalms." It articulates a desperate cry for God's mercy.

Often during the season of Lent people make a concerted effort to do things they do not normally do—like praying, reading the Bible, doing charity work, attending church services, or being less grumpy. Others make concerted efforts to abstain from things they enjoy—like dessert, television, Facebook, or alcoholic beverages.

While these things are fine, they often turn our focus to ourselves rather than to God. Lent is not about what we do or don't do for God. Lent is about remembering what God *has done* for us. Psalm 51 points us to what we need more than anything else in the world, the mercy of God.

Psalm 51 was written by King David. David is known to be the greatest king in the history of Israel. David was the youngest son of Jesse. He was rejected by his father and rejected by his brothers, but chosen by God. When the prophet Samuel was led by the Lord to visit Jesse and anoint one of his sons as the next king of Israel, Jesse invited all his sons except David. David was like the one kid in the neighborhood who was not invited to a birthday party, except it was not his neighbors who snubbed him, it was his family.

But the Lord passed on all David's older brothers, and so Samuel asked Jesse if he had any more sons, and Jesse replied, "There remains yet the youngest, but he is keeping the sheep." Samuel responded, "Send and bring him." David arrived and the Lord told Samuel, "Rise and anoint him for this is the one" and Scripture tells that "the spirit of the Lord came mightily upon David" (1 Samuel 16:1-13).

David went on to defeat Goliath. He led Israel to victory over their oppressors, the Philistines. He later defeated the Philistines again and brought the Ark of the Covenant back to Jerusalem. He wrote many of the Psalms that have been used in worship for thousands of years. David won battles over the Edomites, Moabites, Ammonites, Amalekites, and Philistines. David was the consummate warrior-poet.

He was eventually crowned king of Judah, and seven years later he was crowned king of all Israel—and he reigned for a total of forty years. Moreover, God made a covenant with David and promised that someday a descendant of his would establish a kingdom that would last forever. Listen to what God spoke to David through the prophet, Nathan:

> I will raise up your offspring after you, who shall come forth from your body… and I will establish the throne of his kingdom forever. I will be a father to him and he shall be a son to me… your throne will be established forever (2 Samuel 7:12-16).

David had everything you could ask for: power, wealth, prestige, fame, honor, a huge family, and beyond all that David was anointed with the spirit of God. In short, David was *the* man. But David was also just *a* man, and in 2 Samuel 11 we see that, during the season when kings usually went to war, David stayed home. He had an affair with a married woman named Bathsheba, and when she conceived, David made arrangements for her husband, Uriah the Hittite, who was out fighting battles against the Ammonites on David's behalf, to be abandoned in the heat of battle so that he would be killed. King David, the man after God's own heart, the one anointed with the spirit of God, committed adultery and murder.

David tried to do what many of us do when we sin, he tried to cover it up, but it didn't work. For the same prophet, Nathan, through whom God had earlier spoken his promise of establishing an everlasting kingdom, came once again to David, this time to confront him with his sin. At this point, however, David stopped trying to cover up his sin, and he responded to Nathan with one simple sentence: "I have sinned against the Lord."

David no longer tried to cover up his sin. He made no excuses. He did not say, "Oh well, boys will be boys." He did not say, "I did not have sex with that woman." He did not tell Nathan that his childhood experiences of rejection made him especially vulnerable to temptation. He did not ask to appear on Dr. Phil. Instead, David owned up to the reality of his sin. David in this case would have agreed with the classic song written by blues legend Blind Willie Johnson (and later covered by Led Zeppelin), "Nobody's Fault but Mine." David's response to Nathan was a plainly honest self-assessment: "I have sinned against the Lord."

This was the darkest and most stressful season in David's life. He had not been this stressed when walking across the field to face Goliath. He had not been this stressed when fleeing for his life from King Saul. He had not been this stressed in the many times he had been in battle. I imagine David experienced what we confess about our sins in the confession each week: "the remembrance of them is grievous unto us, the burden of them is intolerable" *(BCP, 331)*.

David turned to God, the same God who had chosen him, delivered him time and time again, and anointed him with the Spirit. David turned to God and prayed what became known as Psalm 51: "Have mercy on me, O God."

When David was confronted with the reality and the gravity of his sin he did not appeal to his Lenten disciplines, he appealed to the grace of God: "Have mercy on me, O God, *according to your loving-kindness; in your great compassion* blot out my transgressions." David surely remembered that when God revealed himself to Moses on Mt. Sinai he proclaimed, "The Lord, the Lord, a God merciful and gracious, slow to anger, and abounding in steadfast love and faithfulness" (Exodus 34:6). David appealed to the grace of God.

And David continued, "Wash me through and through from my wickedness and cleanse me from my sin." David experienced the truth of what the prophet Jeremiah was to preach years later: "The heart is devious above all else; it is perverse—who can understand it?" (Jeremiah 17:9). David experienced the truth of what Jesus preached many years after that: "For out of the heart come evil intentions, murder, adultery, fornication, theft, false witness, slander. These are what defile a person" (Matthew 15:19-20a). David knew that only God could wash him "through and through" and cleanse him from his sin. David, the man after God's own heart, knew that God looks at the heart (1 Samuel 16:7) and he knew that what was in his heart could only be cleansed by God. And so David appealed to the grace of God.

And God had mercy on David and forgave him. And although David had to deal with the fallout of his sin in the life of his family, *God* forgave him, and *God* kept his promise: for many years later a descendant of David was indeed born, rejected by men but chosen by God (1 Peter 2:4). In Jesus Christ, the King of Kings, God kept his promise made to David.

Through his death on the cross Jesus Christ atoned for the sins of everyone in the world, including David, and including you and me. The death and resurrection of Jesus Christ is the closing statement of what is referred to in Psalm 51 as the "loving-kindness" and "great compassion" of God.

Through trust in Jesus Christ our sins are forgiven, our offenses are blotted out. It's as if God opened a document on his computer that listed every single sin in our lives, and then typed "Ctrl + A" to shade them all, "Delete" to delete them all, and "Ctrl + S" to save the change—so that when God opens the document that *once* listed all our sins he now sees a blank document. Through faith in Jesus Christ we are justified, our sins are blotted out by the precious blood of Jesus Christ.

And not only does the blood of Jesus Christ blot out our sins, it also cleanses us "through and through." That happens when we confess our sins to God, as John wrote in his first letter: "If we confess our sins, he who is faithful and just will forgive us our sins and cleanse us from all unrighteousness" (1 John 1:9).

When David, the man after God's own heart, the greatest king in Israel's history, found himself at the end of his rope because of his sin, he turned to the only One to whom he could turn, God, and asked for the only thing that could save him, mercy. David expressed that in Psalm 51, and we too, when we find ourselves at the end of our rope because of sin, can pray Psalm 51 and ask God for mercy. When it is all said and done, we need God's mercy more than anything else, and God gives us that mercy in Jesus Christ. That is the good news of the Gospel.

I recently read *Foxe's Book of Martyrs*, written by John Foxe and originally published in 1563. It is a classic and moving account of the heroic suffering and death of many Christian martyrs, with particular emphasis on those burned at the stake during the English Reformation, and as such is a stirring reminder of our heritage as Christians in the Anglican tradition.

On February 9, 1555 an Anglican priest named Rowland Taylor, who served as Rector of Hadleigh in Suffolk, was burned at the stake for his Protestant convictions. In addition to being respected by his parish, Taylor was loved by his wife, Mary, and their nine children. Five days before his death he wrote the following to his wife and children:

> I believe that they are blessed which die in the Lord. God careth for sparrows and for the hairs of our heads. I have ever found him more faithful and favorable, than is any father or husband. Trust ye therefore in him by the means of our dear Savior Christ's merits: believe, love, fear, and obey him: pray to him, for he hath promised to help. Count me not dead, for I shall certainly live, and never die. I go before, and you shall follow after, to our long home.

At about 2:00AM on the day of his death Taylor was taken from his cell and his wife, Mary, and two of his daughters, Mary and Elizabeth, who had suspected this might happen and had waited outside, ran up to him. The sheriff granted Taylor a few moments with his family. The four of them held one another, knelt and prayed the Lord's Prayer, while the sheriff wept. John Foxe continues:

> After they had prayed, (Taylor) rose up and kissed his wife... and said, 'Farewell my dear wife, and be of good comfort, for I am quiet in my conscience. God shall stir up a father for our children.' And then he kissed his daughter, Mary, and said, 'God bless thee and make thee his servant:' and kissing Elizabeth, he said, 'God bless thee; I pray you all stand strong and steadfast unto Christ and his Word.'

As Taylor was tied to the stake later that day, awaiting his painful death, guess what he was reciting? Psalm 51: "Have mercy on me, O God, according to your loving-kindness; in your great compassion blot out my offenses. Wash me through and through from my wickedness and cleanse me from my sin." Rowland Taylor, at death's doorstep, asked God for mercy. When it is all said and done, it is only the mercy of God, the grace of God in Jesus Christ that can save us. Taylor knew that it is the merits of Jesus Christ that saves us, not our own efforts.

If today you are in a place in your life in which you realize your need for the mercy of God, if you are in a "Nobody's Fault but Mine" frame of mind, you do not have to wait until you are at the end of your rope like David or at death's doorstep like Rowland Taylor to ask God for mercy. You can ask God for mercy right now: "Have mercy on me, O God, according to your loving-kindness; in your great compassion blot out my offenses. Wash me through and through from my wickedness and cleanse me from my sin."

Lent is not about what you do or don't do for God. It is about what God has already done for you in Jesus Christ. In Jesus Christ and his atoning death on the cross God has given you what you need more than anything else, his mercy.

And his mercy is more than enough.

Amen.

GOD IS A RESTORING GOD
Charcoal Fires and the Brand New Start

Jesus said to them, "Come and have breakfast."
Now none of the disciples dared to ask him,
"Who are you?" because they knew it was the
Lord (John 21:12).

In the Name of the Father, Son, and Holy Spirit.

In the summer of 2003 my wife and I saw *Seabiscuit,* a film
that shows us what restoration looks like. Based on a true
story, it recounts how a racehorse named Seabiscuit that had
been written off after injury, is physically restored, and goes
on to win stunning victory after stunning victory. By the end
of Seabiscuit's career the horse had become at that point the
all-time leading money winner in racing history, and went on
to sire 108 foals. Seabiscuit's story of restoration became a
source of encouragement and inspiration during the Great

Depression. I am very moved by that film because it brings to life what we see in today's Gospel passage from John 21, wherein Jesus restores Peter.

We live in a throwaway culture. The Environmental Protection Agency reports that the United States produces about 220 million tons of garbage each year, which would cover more than 82,000 football fields six feet deep in compacted garbage. In spite of all the current recycling efforts, when things get used or broken we tend to throw them away. Unfortunately this is not only the case with impersonal things like cars, clothes, furniture, and cell phones, but also deeply personal things like friendships and convictions. Our world is full of people and relationships thrown away like flotsam and jetsam. The good news is that although *we* live in a throwaway culture, God is *not* a throwaway God.

God is a restoring God.

One of my favorite websites is dictionary.com, from which I receive a daily "word of the day" e-mail. *Restore* is defined as: "bringing back into existence or use; bringing back to a former, original, or normal condition, bringing back to a state of health, soundness, or vigor; putting back to a former place, or to a former position." To restore means to bring something back to the way it ought to be. Because of the death and resurrection of Jesus Christ, God does these things for us. God restores us as he restored Peter.

In John 21 we see that some of the disciples are together again. Jesus has appeared to them twice. They have seen his scars. Even Thomas now believes. And yet Peter is still plagued with guilt about what he had done in denying Jesus three times in his darkest hour. As far as his standing with Jesus went, Peter considered himself a failure. So Peter does what many of us do when we feel like a failure—he returns to what he knows. He goes fishing. "I am going fishing," he tells his fellow disciples, several of whom join him.

They fish all night long, and catch absolutely nothing.

That's when Jesus shows up. At dawn the disciples dimly see someone standing on the shore. This person calls out and asked them if they had caught anything, to which the disciples answer bluntly, "No." Then Jesus tells them, "Cast your net to the right side of the boat, and you will find some." Peter and the other disciples are seasoned fisherman. After being out fishing all night I imagine the last thing they want are helpful suggestions.

Nevertheless the disciples cast the net off the right side of their boat and catch so many fish they're unable to haul it in. After goose egging on fish all night, the disciples in a matter of minutes haul in 153 fish. It is at this point that John recognizes that the man calling out to them from the shore is none other than the risen Jesus Christ.

Sometimes in our lives we go through seasons in which we give everything we have to something and see very little or no results. And then there are the seasons when God intervenes and you can hardly keep up with all the ways he blesses you. This was the case in one of my favorite movies, *Forrest Gump*. After coming home from Vietnam, Forrest— per the suggestion from his friend, Bubba—moves to the Gulf Coast to start the Bubba Gump Shrimp Company. Lieutenant Dan later joins him, and the two spend weeks trying to catch shrimp, but catch only a few. Mostly their nets are filled with garbage—boots, toilet seats, license plates—with only a few shrimp. Then, after an act of God, in the form of a hurricane they catch so many shrimp they cannot keep up with the inflow.

The same thing happens here with the disciples. They fish all night for nothing. Jesus intervenes and they can hardly contain their catch. After John recognizes Jesus, Peter, like Forrest Gump, jumps out of the boat to swim to Jesus as fast as he can.

Jesus asks Peter and the others to bring some of the fish they had caught, and simply says, "Come and have breakfast." Jesus knew that after being out fishing all night the disciples were probably very hungry, so he makes breakfast for them. This shows the tender concern Jesus has for his disciples, now gathered around the charcoal fire, eating the breakfast he has personally prepared for them.

Then Jesus restores Peter.

After they eat, Jesus, in front of the other disciples, directly addresses the issue that had been weighing Peter down, his guilt about having denied him three times. Peter was feeling down and out. In the early 1900's an American songwriter named Jimmy Cox wrote a song called, "Nobody Knows You When You're Down and Out," which later became a popular song during the Great Depression. Clapton later covered it on his Grammy-winning 1992 *Unplugged* album:

> Nobody knows you
> When you're down and out.
> In your pocket, not one penny
> And as for friends, you don't have any.
>
> When you finally get back up on your feet again
> Everybody wants to be your old long-lost friend
> Said it's mighty strange, without a doubt
> Nobody knows you when you're down and out.

The good news of the Gospel is that even if "nobody knows you when you're down and out," God does. In fact, God knows you *above all* when you are down and out. When Peter was down and out, Jesus meets him right there and restores him. Jesus isn't waffling, he is compassionately *specific* about how—and where—he restores Peter.

Jesus restores Peter as he sits in front of a charcoal fire. This is significant because, the night in which Peter had denied Jesus three times, he did so while warming himself in front of a charcoal fire. By intentionally restoring him here, Jesus gives Peter a tangible sign of his grace.

Jesus also addresses Peter as "Simon," Peter's original name. Near the beginning of John's account of the Gospel Andrew brings this Simon to Jesus, who says to him, "You are Simon son of John. You are to be called Cephas (which is translated Peter)" (John 1:42). Cephas means "Rock." Similarly when Simon Peter correctly identifies Jesus as the Son of God at Caesarea Philippi, Jesus responded, "Blessed are you, Simon... I tell you, you are Peter, and on this rock I will build my church, and the gates of Hades will not prevail against it" (Matthew 16:17-18). Jesus knew that Peter, having denied him three times, felt like anything but a rock, and certainly felt that the gates of hell had prevailed against him, rather than the other way around. And so Jesus meets Peter right there and addresses him as "Simon."

Then Jesus asks him, "Simon, Son of John, do you love me?" Jesus asks Peter this question three times, the same number of times Peter had denied him. He gives Peter three chances to proclaim his love for the One whom he had denied. God is not just a God of second chances. God gives Peter *multiple* chances, and he does the same for you and me. Even though Peter has denied Jesus, Jesus will not deny Peter. God is always faithful to us, even when we're unfaithful to him. In his second Letter to Timothy, Paul writes, "if we are faithless, he remains faithful—for he cannot deny himself" (2:13).

Not only does Jesus give Peter three opportunities to proclaim his love for him, he also gives him three charges: "Feed my lambs... Tend my sheep... Feed my sheep." In other words, "Peter, care for my followers." Jesus reinstates Peter as a servant in his church. God is not a throwaway God. God is a restoring God.

In the Parable of the Prodigal Son (Luke 15:11-32) Jesus emphasizes that God is a restoring God as he describes how the rebellious son is completely restored by his father. When the rebellious son finally returns home after squandering his inheritance on lusty living and selfishness, the father not only throws a welcome home party, he also gives his son three things: a robe signifying that he was the restored guest of honor, a ring signifying his restored authority, and sandals signifying his restored position as his son. The gracious father gives his son these three things in the presence of his family and friends.

Jesus graciously gives Peter the same full restoration in the presence of his disciples. Jesus restores him before a charcoal fire like the one where he denied him. He addresses him as "Simon," knowing he felt like anything but a rock. He gives him three opportunities to proclaim his love for him. He charges him three times to care for his sheep. In short, Jesus gives Peter a brand new start.

This restored Peter, only weeks later, preaches a sermon on Pentecost to thousands of people. This restored Peter preaches the Gospel throughout the Roman Empire, endures persecution over the course of his apostolic ministry, is eventually martyred under Nero, choosing to be crucified upside-down because he did not consider himself worthy to die like the One who had restored him. Peter, who had been called by Jesus to be "the Rock," only to be the unfaithful one in the Lord's darkest hour, is fully restored by Jesus.

How about you today? Perhaps guilt or the feeling of failure weighs you down, like Peter at the beginning of today's Gospel passage. Perhaps you feel like you've been thrown away like so many other things in our culture. Or maybe you feel like you've been fishing all night in some way in your life and can't catch anything. Maybe you find yourself in the midst of a hurricane.

In John 21 the good news is that God restores, tenderly, compassionately, completely. As Bruce Milne writes in *The Message of John*, "No matter how desperate our failure, or how deep-seated our shame, (God) can forgive and renew us and then use us in his service. Failure is never final with God" (p. 317).

The good news is that through his death on the cross Jesus restores all of us, like he did Peter. Jesus Christ, the Son of God, was thrown out by the ones he came to save. Nobody wanted to know Jesus when he was down and out, naked, abandoned, and crucified. And yet he dies for us. Jesus is thrown away on our behalf. This same Jesus is raised on the third day, and our standing with God has been restored. Because of his resurrection we have the sure and certain hope that one day all things will be fully restored in Jesus Christ.

The good news is that in Jesus Christ God gives us what Jesus gave Peter in today's passage: a brand new start. God is not a throwaway God; God is a restoring God.

Amen.

JUSTIFIED BY FAITH
Why Nuns and Trashcans Never Worked for Springsteen

We know that a person is justified not by the works of the law but through faith in Jesus Christ. And we have come to believe in Christ Jesus, so that we might be justified by faith in Christ, and not by doing the works of the law, because no one will be justified by the works of the law (Galatians 2:16).

In the Name of the Father, Son, and Holy Spirit.

One of the hallmarks of Protestant theology is *justification by faith*. In today's reading from Paul's Letter to the Galatians, *justification by faith* is precisely the main point. Justification by faith means that we are made righteous in God's eyes by nothing more than *faith* in Jesus Christ. We are not justified by what we do, but by what we *trust* God has already done for us in the death of Jesus Christ on the cross.

The legendary coach John Wooden recently died at the age of 99. Last week I was watching the NBA Finals with my son and, during the halftime show, one of Wooden's former players from UCLA, Hall of Famer Bill Walton, was reminiscing about Wooden's famous sayings. The one he emphasized was priceless: "It's what you learn *after* you know it all that counts."

This was the case with the Apostle Paul, who was a Jew from Tarsus, a Roman citizen who had received the best education possible for a Jewish young man. Tutored by the renowned rabbi Gamaliel, Paul was a rising star among the Pharisees, who emphasized obedience to and justification by the laws of the Hebrews. Paul took great pride in his obedience to the law. He describes this in his Letter to the Philippians:

> If anyone else has reason to be confident in the flesh, I have more: circumcised on the eighth day, a member of the people of Israel, of the tribe of Benjamin, a Hebrew born of Hebrews; as to the law, a Pharisee; as to zeal, a persecutor of the church; as to righteousness under the law, blameless (3:4b-6).

Paul was so zealous for the law that he persecuted Christians, those who believed in Jesus Christ, the fulfiller of the law. Paul's persecution of Christians did not consist of blistering blog posts or Twitter feeds, but instead in the separating of loved ones, the imprisonment and execution of believing Christians. For Paul righteousness through the works of the law was no religious hobbyhorse, it was the be-all-end-all of life. When it came to righteousness through the works of the law, Paul in fact knew it all.

But just like John Wooden said, "It's what you learn *after* you know it all that counts." After his life-changing encounter with the risen Jesus Christ on the road to Damascus, Paul learns something that counts more than any of the law-zeal he formerly knew: that we are justified through *faith* in Jesus Christ alone, as he wrote to the church in Philippi:

> Yet whatever gains I had, these I have come to regard as loss because of Christ... For his sake I have suffered the loss of all things, and I regard them as rubbish, in order that I may gain Christ and be found in him, not having a righteousness of my own that comes from the law, but one that comes through faith in Christ, the righteousness from God based on faith (3:7-9).

And that is it for Paul. He spends the rest of his life traveling the Roman Empire, preaching the Gospel—justification through faith in Jesus Christ—planting churches, and suffering for the sake of Christ. He authors thirteen of the twenty-seven books of the New Testament, and a recurring theme in all of them is justification through faith. It is what Paul learns after he knows it all that counted.

And it's the same with us. We live in a myriad of meritocracies, a culture of judgers and provers. This past week I attended both a fifth grade graduation and an eighth grade graduation, and the number of awards given out was crazy. The classic is the Perfect Attendance Award—I always feel a little sorry for the kids who can't stay home even if they're sick (and the other kids at school who take his germs home with them).

Of course the meritocracy doesn't stop in eighth grade. It's the way the world works. But when it comes to our salvation, when it comes to being justified by faith, it's what we learn *after* we know it all that counts. We are not saved by our merits or justified by works. We are justified solely through faith in Jesus Christ.

One of my heroes is Thomas Cranmer, the Archbishop of Canterbury and leading figure of the English Reformation. He wrote and compiled the first and second English prayer books (1549 and 1552). Cranmer, along with some others, wrote some sermons that were compiled into two *Books of Homilies*. Listen to how Cranmer describes justification by faith in his sermon entitled "A Sermon of the Salvation of Mankind by Only Christ Our Saviour from Sin and Death Everlasting" (quite a title):

> This justification or righteousness, which we so receive by God's mercy and Christ's merits, embraced by faith, is taken, accepted, and allowed of God for our perfect and full justification... For all the good works that we can do be imperfect, and therefore not able to deserve our justification: but our justification doth come freely, by the mere mercy of God; and of so great and free mercy that, whereas all the world was not able of their selves to pay any part towards their ransom, it pleased our heavenly Father, of his infinite mercy, without any our desert or deserving, to prepare for us the most precious jewels of Christ's body and blood, whereby our ransom might be fully paid, the law fulfilled, and his justice fully satisfied. So that Christ is now the righteousness of all them that truly do believe in him. He for them paid their ransom by his death. He for them fulfilled the law in his life.

Cranmer did not retire comfortably with a generous pension for archbishops, juggling speaking engagements with trips to see his grandkids. In fact, at the age of sixty-six on a rainy Saturday morning, March 21, 1556, he was dragged from the pulpit at St. Mary's Church in Oxford as he was preaching and driven to the center of town where he was burned at the stake for his convictions. Justification by faith is a life and death matter.

And our justification is due solely and completely to the mercy of God, a mercy Cranmer described as "great," "free," and "infinite."

After I graduated from college I worked in finance for a while... as a bank teller. I worked at a bank in Northern Virginia, on King St. in Alexandria. It was a fascinating and humbling place to work. I was the only white male who worked there, and the vast majority of our customers were immigrants from Africa, Asia, and the Middle East. I'm not exactly a financial wizard, so I learned a lot of helpful things. One day an elderly man from Vietnam came in and walked up to my window. "Deposit!" he cried as he slammed his check on the counter. There was no deposit slip and no account number on the check, so I replied, "Yes, sir—savings account or checking account?" "No!" he yelled, "Deposit!" I repeated my response and he got really fired up and started yelling, "Deposit! Deposit! Deposit!" as he jumped up and down, slamming his hand on the counter. Our head teller, a very kind woman from the Philippines named Layla (she was born before the Derek and the Dominos classic song) spoke Vietnamese and called the gentleman over and politely completed his deposit. From then on, every time he entered the bank, he would glare at me and would only go to Layla's window.

In the fourth chapter of his Letter to the Romans Paul describes how the righteousness of God is credited to our account through faith in Jesus Christ. In other words, because of our sin we owe a debt to God that we can never repay—no matter how well we do keeping the law, no matter how great our merits—we can't pay the debt we owe because of our sin. But God in his grace, God in his great, free, and infinite mercy, paid that debt for us through the death of

Jesus Christ on the cross to atone for our sins. Through faith in him, God's righteousness is placed in our account. It is a free gift of God, a check of forgiveness that is placed in our account, a check of forgiveness that covers all our sins. It is deposited through faith; no yelling necessary.

Faith itself is a gift of God. Scripture tells us that God gives each of us a "measure of faith" (Romans 12:3), or as Roland Bainton wrote in his classic biography of Martin Luther, *Here I Stand*: "Faith is not an achievement. It is a gift." And we are not only justified by faith, by belief and trust in the grace and mercy of God, but we live our lives by faith as well, as Scripture tells us, "The just shall live by faith" (Romans 1:17, KJV).

I recently read Jon Krakauer's *Into the Wild*, in which he recounts some of his mountaineering experiences, including solo ascents of icy Alaskan peaks. Listen to how he felt during these climbs thousands of feet high:

> All that held me to the mountainside, all that held me to the world, were two thin spikes of chrome stuck half an inch into a smear of frozen water... early on a climb, especially a difficult solo climb, you constantly feel the abyss pulling at your back... the siren song of the void puts you on edge; it makes your movements tentative, clumsy, herky-jerky.

Sometimes our faith, the only thing holding us to the mountainside, feels that small. Sometimes the circumstances in our lives get really hard—we can feel the abyss pulling at our backs and hear the siren song of the void, our minds riddled with anxiety and fear.

But that small spike of faith is plenty; faith in Jesus Christ, whose death on the cross atoned for all. It is faith in Jesus Christ, the Lamb of God who takes away the sin of the world that saves us (John 1:29). And that faith is a gift from God, which means that even if the thin spikes of chrome that are holding us to the mountainside break, and we think we are falling into the void, God will catch us. Jesus, referring to himself as the Good Shepherd and you and me as the sheep, said: "I give them eternal life, and they will never perish. No one will snatch them out of my hand" (John 10:28). We are justified by faith in the One who will never let us go.

In the late fifties to early sixties there was a boy who attended Catholic schools. When he was in third grade and acted out of line in class, a nun stuffed him into the garbage can under her desk and told him that's where he belonged. As an altar boy during Mass he made a mistake once and a priest knocked him down the stairs leading up to the altar. The young man was Bruce Springsteen (see *It Ain't No Sin to be Glad You're Alive: The Promise of Bruce Springsteen* by Eric Alterman).

And yet in spite of all that Springsteen has written many inspiring songs over the past forty years, including "Badlands," the classic opening track from his brilliant 1978 album, *Darkness on the Edge of Town*, in which he sings:

> I believe in the love that you gave me.
> I believe in the faith that could save me.
> I believe in the hope and I pray that someday it
> Will raise me above these Badlands...

The good news of the Gospel is that we are justified by faith in Jesus Christ and his death on the cross for us. We can believe in the love he gives us and this faith saves us. It is a hope assuring us that we will not only be raised not only above our current badlands but from the grave itself. The good news of the Gospel is that, regardless of whether you've been put in trashcans or knocked down stairs by the very ones from whom you should have received love and encouragement, you *are* loved. You are loved by the One who was knocked down repeatedly on the way to Calvary. You are loved by the One who was nailed to the cross to atone for our sins. You are loved by the One who paid the debt we could never ever pay.

Well, enough about John Wooden, the kids with perfect attendance, Thomas Cranmer, deposit man, Jon Krakauer, and Bruce Springsteen—what about you? Where are you feeling the need to justify or escape justice? Where do you need reassurance about your standing?

You can be assured for the first time or reassured yet again that you are fully known and fully loved, that you are forgiven, that God will never let you go, that your debt to God has been fully paid and deposited into your account.

You can be encouraged by the Gospel that you are justified solely through faith in Jesus Christ, not by anything you can or can't do.

Amen.

DISTRACTED
Mary, Martha and the Better Portion

Now as they went on their way, he entered a certain village, where a woman named Martha welcomed him into her home. She had a sister named Mary, who sat at the Lord's feet and listened to what he was saying. But Martha was distracted by her many tasks; so she came to him and asked, "Lord, do you not care that my sister has left me to do all the work by myself? Tell her then to help me." But the Lord answered her, "Martha, Martha, you are worried and distracted by many things; there is need of only one thing. Mary has chosen the better part, which will not be taken away from her" (Luke 10:38-42).

In the Name of the Father, Son, and Holy Spirit.

This week I'm preaching about Jesus' visit with Martha and Mary. Luke is the only one of the four Gospel writers who records this episode.

Jesus and his disciples are welcomed into the home of a woman named Martha, who lives with her younger sister, Mary, in the small town of Bethany. Martha graciously welcomes Jesus and his disciples into her home and begins scurrying about, doing various tasks that hosts are expected to do. She is the dutiful older sibling. Meanwhile, her younger sister, Mary, simply sits at Jesus' feet, listening to what he is saying.

Perhaps you have experienced these dynamics in your house—someone busily getting done what *needs* to get done while others in the have taken it upon themselves to, well, chill out. I imagine Martha being a gracious host, meticulously tending to her tablecloths and placemats—but her attention was not on Jesus. Luke tells us that Martha was "distracted by her many tasks."

Can you relate?

Have you seen this TV show called *Wipeout?* In this show contestants put on a helmet and proceed to complete "the world's largest obstacle course." *Wipeout* is not so much about the obstacles themselves, but about the distractions that await you as you try to complete it. These distractions include the "Sucker Punch" (a wall with random punching gloves), "Spikes of Doom" (a swinging wall of spikes), and "Sweeper Arms" (large pillars rotating like helicopter blades). Nobody completes the obstacle course without getting knocked off their feet by these completely ridiculous distractions.

The problem is, no matter how ridiculous, distractions do tend to knock us off our feet. It's very real that, often, while trying to complete the routine obstacles in our lives, it is the distractions that often cause pain; as the Canadian singer-songwriter Bruce Cockburn sings in "The Whole Night Sky": "Sometimes a wind comes out of nowhere and knocks you sideways. And look, see my tears, they fill the whole night sky."

Martha is distracted by many things. Jesus Christ himself is in her house and she is still frenetically running about, thinking the whole time that she *is* serving him, that she *is* providing him with the kind of hospitality he is looking for, but she's not. In fact, it's her younger sister, Mary, the one apparently *not* so busy, the one who is *not* scurrying about, the one who is *not* doing *anything*—it is Mary—*really?*—who is offering Jesus the kind of hospitality he is looking for?

This greatly annoys Martha, and understandably so, because Mary is just *sitting* there. Mary is annoyed with Jesus because *apparently* he doesn't care. In her busyness Martha has become completely self-centered. Her efforts were not really focused on providing hospitality for Jesus, but on getting done what she wanted to get done. This self-centeredness is clear in what she tells Jesus: "Lord, do you not care that *my* sister has left *me* to do all the work by *myself?* Tell her then to help *me.*"

And how does Jesus respond to Martha? He does not say, "You're right, Martha. Mary *is* a slacker; if only she could be as productive as you." He does not rebuke Mary, "How can you just sit there while your sister does all the work?" Instead, Jesus responds: "Martha, Martha, you are worried and distracted by many things."

Jesus repeats her name, "Martha, Martha," to show that his focus is entirely on her, to show that he in fact does care, to show his compassion, and then he cuts to the heart of what's really going on in Martha's life: "you are worried and distracted by many things." Martha's fatigue and irritability are not rooted in her efforts to provide hospitality; nor are they rooted in her annoyance with Mary or Jesus; her fatigue and irritability are rooted in the worries and distractions of her life.

Martha struggled inwardly with worry and outwardly with distractions. Can you relate?

Have you ever gone on vacation to "get away from it all" only to find out that "it all" follows you? That's because we cannot get away from the inward worries that we all have. They don't leave us alone. They just keep hounding us, even on vacation, just like in the hilarious 1991 film, *What About Bob?* in which the neurotic Bob Wiley (Bill Murray) hounds his stressed-out psychiatrist, Dr. Leo Marvin (Richard Dreyfuss). Dr. Marvin goes on vacation to New Hampshire, delighted to leave all his worries back in New York, including Bob Wiley, but Wiley finds him and never goes away. Ultimately Dr. Marvin goes crazy and Bob Wiley is "cured" and ends up marrying Dr. Marvin's sister and becoming a permanent part of his family.

If I were to ask you to tell me today what you are worried about, what would you tell me?

Every week people talk to me about the things in their lives that cause worry—a frightening medical diagnosis, family dysfunction, a marriage on the rocks, a child in trouble, doubts about their faith, a secret addiction, self-hatred, a major financial setback.

We have umpteen different things to help us live supposedly more productive lives but often they simply create more distractions. For example, a phone that you not only use for talking but for taking photos, recording video, watching movies, playing music, checking email, with hundreds of apps to utilize. I was recently riding in a new hybrid car a couple months ago with a friend and, on the dashboard was a computer animation of his engine, with all the fluid levels, miles per gallon ratios he was getting at that precise speed, outside temperature, inside temperature, etc. My friend laughed and turned it off—"It's pretty cool," he said, "but distracting."

And just like people talk to me each week about things that worry them they also talk to me about bigger distractions, distractions that carry much greater consequences than phone apps or dashboard monitors—kids distracted by what others think of them, and the temptations to drugs and alcohol; people whose marriage is not in a good place, distracted by unexpected feelings for someone other than their spouse; employees distracted by what looks like a more enticing job possibility; people distracted by false cures for the pain in their lives—alcohol, pornography, materialism—that ultimately create only more pain. These distractions can repeatedly knock us sideways.

And in the same way we cannot escape our inward worries by going on vacation we cannot escape our outward distractions either. A couple weeks ago I was on the Christ Church Habitat for Humanity trip to West Virginia. The two dozen guys on the trip slept in a single bunk room, and at night there were times when it was a veritable symphony of snoring. One night I awoke about 3:00 and could not get back to sleep because the snoring was so loud, so I took my sleeping bag to the upstairs meeting room to crash on a couch. One of our other guys was already in the room, soundly sleeping on one of the other couches. I read for awhile and eventually went back to sleep. When I awoke the other guy was gone, and I thought nothing of it. Later that week I found out that he had originally gone up there for the same reason I had, to escape the snoring and try to get back to sleep. Although he was asleep when I got there, after I fell asleep, guess who's snoring woke him up? He told me he was freaking out—there was no escape from the snoring—so he just went back to the bunkroom and made the best of it while I slept and snored away. Talk about "no rest for the weary." There is just no escaping the distractions in our lives.

But the good news is that Jesus meets us in that place, in the midst of the worries and distractions of our lives, with care and compassion, just like he did with Martha: "Martha, Martha, you are worried and distracted by many things."

And then Jesus, ironically enough, points Martha to her sister, Mary. "There is need of only one thing," Jesus tells her, "Mary has chosen the better part, which will not be taken away from her." (I'm sure Martha felt really blessed by that.)

While Martha is running amok, trying to serve Jesus, worried and distracted, Mary simply sits at Jesus' feet, listening to him, and *that* was the kind of hospitality Jesus was looking for.

Mary chooses the better part. Mary is drawn not only into who Jesus is, but also to what he is saying, and she felt compelled to sit and listen. Have you ever read a book that you can't put down? Have you ever been in a rich conversation with a friend that you wished would never end? Have you ever been driving and heard a song on the radio that is so good you have to listen to the whole thing, even if it means waiting in your car in your driveway until it ends? Have you ever walked outside at the end of a workday and been stopped in your tracks by a stunningly beautiful evening sky or sunset? When something really resonates with us, when something touches us in our hearts, when something ministers life to us, sometimes, just like Mary, we can do nothing else but sit and take it in.

Luke is silent about what Jesus was talking about with Mary and the disciples, but obviously was ministering life to her, and she simply sat there and listened. Apparently Jesus was not yelling at her and telling her what was wrong with her life. On the TV show, *The Office*, Michael Scott describes his view on what an intervention is: "An intervention is sort of hard to describe, but really it's a surprise party for people who have addictions. And you get in their face and you scream at them and you make them feel really bad about themselves. And then they stop." Jesus is not performing that kind of intervention. Instead, he is speaking words of life to Mary.

During the Great Depression a young boy from a poor farming family in Arkansas spent his days working the cotton fields and his nights listening to the radio. He could not stop listening to the music. His father was a hard man, scarred by the pressures and pains of life. He, like Martha, was worried and distracted by many things. He thought his son's love for music was an utter waste of time. But his son, like Mary, could not stop listening to the radio. The music resonated deep within him. The music ministered life to him. That boy was Johnny Cash, who became a music legend, whose songs have resonated on the radio with millions of people, and when he was inducted in the Country Music Hall of Fame in 1980, his dad was sitting in the front row. Although with regards to his love for music Johnny Cash's dad was originally like Martha, eventually he became more like Mary, eventually he chose the better part.

So what happened to Martha and Mary after this episode? Luke is silent about this. In fact, Luke never mentions Martha and Mary again—but John the Evangelist does. In John's account of the Gospel we see that late in Jesus' ministry this same Martha and Mary had a brother named Lazarus who died, and Jesus went to see them. While he was on his way, Martha met Him and told him, "Lord, if you had been here my brother would not have died." Jesus then told her, "I am the resurrection and the life… those who believe in me, even though they die, will live… Do you believe this?" And how did Martha respond? "Yes, Lord," she said, "I believe." And as you know, Jesus indeed raised Lazarus from the dead. Later Martha had a dinner party and invited Jesus. And that's when Mary appears on the scene again, this time with costly perfume which she poured on Jesus' feet, which she also wiped with her hair. Mary gave the most valuable thing she owned in grateful worship of Jesus. Mary anointed him ahead of time for his burial.

The better part is a relationship with Jesus Christ, the One who created us and redeemed us; the One who knows us better than we know ourselves and loves us so much that he died for us; the One who understands all the worries and distractions in our lives and, as he did for Martha, meets us with compassion, and calls us by name. Jesus was knocked sideways by our sins, and nailed to a cross, where he atoned for them, all of them. And because Jesus, just as he told Martha, is indeed the resurrection and the life, he gives us the hope of eternal life as well. A relationship with Jesus Christ does not make the worries and distractions go away, but it gives us hope in the midst of them, hope that as Paul wrote to the Colossians, the blood Jesus shed on the cross indeed has and will reconcile all things to himself, including the things that worry and distract us (1:19-20). In the meantime He offers us the better part, a relationship with him.

I'll close with one more story, one I'm sharing with permission. Last week we had a visitor to Christ Church who is from an un-churched background, someone who had questions about Christianity. She was moved by the worship service and wanted to talk, so we met on Thursday and talked for awhile. She told me that although she was happily married and had a good job, she felt like something was missing in her life. I simply explained the basics of the gospel to her—that God created us and loves us, that we are fully known and fully loved, that God loves us so much that he sent his only Son, Jesus Christ, to die on the cross to pay the price for all our sins, that he offers us forgiveness, the Holy Spirit, the hope of eternal life, all as a free gift. She prayed to receive Christ into her life right then, wiping tears from her eyes afterwards. Then she asked about being baptized. We went through the baptism liturgy together from *The Book of Common Prayer* and she was baptized today. Her name is

Jessica, and like Mary, she chose the better part, a relationship with Jesus Christ.

So be encouraged today. If you, like me, are like Martha, "worried and distracted by many things," remember that God loves you as much now as he ever has, and that he offers you anew today the better part, a relationship with him.

Amen.

GOD HAS PAID FOR EVERYTHING
Shakey's Pizza Parlor and the Chop Shop Hero

So if you consider me your partner, welcome him as you would welcome me. If he has wronged you in any way, or owes you anything, charge that to my account (Philemon 17-18).

In the Name of the Father, Son, and Holy Spirit.

I grew up in Northern Virginia, and there was an elderly man in our church we called "Maj." None of us knew his real name, but we knew he had been a major in the U.S. Army and was a veteran of World War II. Everyone looked up to him. A widower of average height, thin and wiry, he always wore the same tweed jacket and fedora, every single Sunday. During the school year on Sundays after church Maj would treat any middle and high school students to the all-you-could-eat buffet at Shakey's Pizza Parlor in Annandale (I don't think it's there anymore). Parents would drop us off at Shakey's after church and pick us up an hour or two later. There were usually about fifteen of us sitting around several tables that had been pushed together, making trip after trip through the buffet line. As a middle school student with a metabolism through the roof, I was in heaven—really, when you're a middle school boy at an all-you-can-eat buffet with a bunch of your goofy friends, does it get any better?

While we were eating, Maj would smile and walk around the tables, talking to each of us, cutting up with us. He always made us feel welcome. I still remember the first time I went, I felt like he was so glad I was there. Maj paid for all of us— the buffet, the drinks, all of it—his treat. I thought there had to be a catch, but there was no catch. Maj welcomed us and paid for everything.

Today I'm preaching from one of the Apostle Paul's lesser-read letters, his Letter to Philemon, the shortest of his thirteen New Testament letters. It's often skipped over. Many people are familiar with Paul's letters to the Romans or Philippians or Corinthians, but not Philemon. Like the Letter of Jude, Philemon is only one chapter, so if you're looking to read an entire book of the Bible in one sitting, it's a good place to start. In fact, you may not know this, but the great nineteenth English novelist Thomas Hardy originally thought of calling his last novel *Philemon the Obscure* instead of *Jude the Obscure* but he didn't think it worked. (Similarly, the Beatles considered entitling their 1968 classic, "Hey Jude," "Hey Philemon," but again, it just didn't seem to fit.) Paul's Letter to Philemon is worth reading because like all his letters, it points us to the Gospel.

Philemon was an elder at the Christian church in Colossae, and Paul's letter was written around the same time he wrote his Letter to the Colossians, which is why in many Bible commentaries Philemon is teamed with Colossians. Philemon had a slave named Onesimus, who had stolen from him and run away to visit Paul in prison. Apparently Paul led Onesimus to become a Christian, because he refers to him as "my child, Onesimus, whose father I have become during my imprisonment."

Paul wrote a Letter to Philemon to encourage him to welcome Onesimus back. It is a personal recommendation letter similar to the recommendation letters that I find myself writing each year for students applying for college or seminary, a personal letter on someone else's behalf.

Although Paul's Letter to Philemon is often overlooked, in it we clearly see the Gospel, particularly in verses 17-18, in which Paul appeals to Philemon, "welcome (Onesimus) as you would welcome me. If he has wronged you in any way, or owes you anything, charge that to my account. I, Paul, am writing this with my own hand: I will repay it." In short, Paul encourages Philemon to welcome Onesimus back and assures him that he would pay for everything.

Paul asks Philemon to welcome Onesimus back as if Onesimus were Paul himself: "welcome (Onesimus) as you would welcome me." Paul and Philemon were good friends as well as brothers in Christ, and Paul knew that if he were released from prison and able to visit Philemon at his home he would be warmly welcomed with much rejoicing and probably a big party, and he asked him to welcome Onesimus back completely, no strings attached. In fact, Paul encourages Philemon to welcome back Onesimus *not* as a slave, but rather as "a beloved brother."

Being welcomed is a major part of the Gospel, as Paul had written to the Romans, "Welcome one another, therefore, just as Christ has welcomed you, for the glory of God" (15:7).

One of the hallmarks of Jesus' earthly ministry was that he welcomed sinners. He ate with them, listened to them, healed them, cared for them, taught them, and was kind to them. Many of the religious leaders hated this about Jesus. In the fifth chapter of the Gospel According to Luke, Jesus is at a banquet in the home of a tax collector named Levi and the Pharisees are furious at him, nitpicking and questioning his motives.

This is how Jesus responds, "Those who are well have no need of a physician, but those who are sick; I have come to call not the righteous but sinners to repentance" (Luke 5:31-32). If you are sick or if you are a sinner, or both, you are in the right place today, because Jesus welcomes sinners. He warmly welcomes them, not as slaves but as beloved brothers and sisters, no strings attached. And the church, the very Body of Christ, is also to be a place of *welcome* for sinners, not some irrelevant club for the self-righteous.

This summer I read a book of poems by T. S. Eliot, including his poem, "Choruses from the Rock." In it he describes how many people consider the church utterly irrelevant to their lives:

> In the pleasant countryside, there it seemed
> That the country now is only fit for picnics.
> And the Church does not seem to be wanted
> In country or in suburb; and in the town
> Only for important weddings.

I am glad that Christ Church is a place where sinners are welcome, not held at arm's length—otherwise I would not be interested in serving here—and I *love* serving here. When I joined the staff here several years ago I was warmly welcomed, even though hardly anyone here knew anything about me, a beautiful example of what it looks like to welcome others as Christ has welcomed us. It's why Christ Church is much more than a historical place for "important weddings."

Throughout scripture Jesus warmly welcomes sinners before they even *think* about getting their act together, because he knows they can *never* get their act together. Jesus welcomes sinners with open arms, open arms that were later stretched to the breaking point and affixed to a cross. Paul is encouraging Philemon to welcome back Onesimus in spite of the fact that he has run away and stolen from him, and to welcome him back as a brother.

Jesus' welcoming sinners is a major part of the Gospel, but it is not the *entire* Gospel, and in his Letter to Philemon Paul not only urges him to welcome Onesimus back as a brother, he also continues: "If he has wronged you in any way, or owes you anything, charge that to my account. I, Paul, am writing this with my own hand: I will repay it."

Paul knows that the issues of running away and theft cannot be overlooked or brushed aside, but must be dealt with head on. Paul does not ask Philemon to overlook the ways Onesimus has wronged him. Paul does not ask him to let bygones be bygones or to "just let it go." Instead, Paul takes Onesimus' burden upon himself: "If he has wronged you in any way," he tells Philemon, "or owes you anything, charge that to *my* account." Paul does not expect Onesimus to bear the burden himself (or to want to) but takes the burden upon himself. The message of the cross is no different—not only does Jesus welcome sinners, he takes the burden of all the ways we have wronged God upon himself and pays everything owed. And he did this for sinners—while we were still sinners, God proved his love for us once and for all in Jesus' death on the cross (Romans 5:8).

In other words, Paul is showing Onesimus the same kind of love he had received from Jesus Christ. The main leader of the Protestant Reformation, Martin Luther, describes this in his *Preface to Paul's Letter to Philemon*:

> What Christ has done for us with God the Father, that St. Paul does also for Onesimus with Philemon. For Christ emptied himself of his rights and overcame the Father with love and humility, so that the Father had to put

away his wrath and rights, and receive us into
favor for the sake of Christ, who so earnestly
advocates our cause and so heartily takes our
part. For we are all his Onesimuses if we
believe.

The reality is that we are all, like Martin Luther says,
"Onesimuses." We have sinned against God, and owe him the
debt of righteousness none of us can ever repay. We, like
Onesimus, have troubled souls.

Arthur Miller's classic 1953 play, *The Crucible*, is about the
1692 Salem witch trials. One of the main characters of the
play is a married farmer named John Proctor, a Puritan who
hated hypocrisy in others but who was also riddled with guilt
because of an affair he had had with Abigail Williams, a
servant on his farm. Listen to how Miller describes him:

> Proctor was a farmer in his middle thirties...
> there is evidence to suggest that he had a
> sharp and biting way with hypocrites... In
> Proctor's presence a fool felt his foolishness
> instantly... But as we shall see, the steady
> manner he displays does not spring from an
> untroubled soul. He is a sinner, a sinner not
> only against the moral fashion of the time,
> but against his own vision of decent conduct.
> These people had no ritual for the washing
> away of sins.

We, like Proctor, loathe the hypocrisy in others and justify
the hypocrisy in ourselves. We have troubled souls, and we
have no ritual for the washing away of sins.

But that is exactly where the Gospel comes in. When Jesus
died on the cross he took our sin upon himself. All the ways
we wronged God and sinned against him were laid on his
account. He fulfilled the law in our place. He made it possible
for troubled souls to be stilled, for people riddled with guilt

to be forgiven and put at ease, for the unwelcomed and unwanted to be welcomed not as slaves, but as beloved brothers and sisters.

Recently my family and I watched the season finale of one of our favorite TV shows, *Friday Night Lights*. Two of the main characters are brothers named Billy and Tim Riggins. The older brother, Billy, and his wife have just had their first child. Desperate for money, Billy starts an illegal business stripping stolen cars and selling the parts piecemeal at a huge profit. Tim allows himself to get sucked into it as well and, of course, eventually the law catches up with them and both are faced with the bleak prospect of a prison sentence.

In this episode the younger brother, Tim, goes to Billy's house, asks him outside, looks him in the eye and says, "I did it. I did it all. You did not do anything… I stripped the cars. I took the money. I took the frames to the junkyard…." Billy, realizing what Tim is about to do, interrupts, "I can't let you do that," to which Tim continues, "You are my brother. You are all I have. You have a family now. You are a father, and you need to be one. This is my decision. This is what I have decided. This is what's going to happen." Billy just starts crying, "I'm sorry. I'm so sorry…" while Tim embraces him. Later Tim and Billy drive to the sheriff's office and Tim gives Billy the keys to his pick-up truck and turns himself in to take Billy's blame upon himself, so that the punishment is paid and Billy, now off the hook, can be free to return to his wife and new son. Tim pays the full price.

That is the resounding message from the cross. Jesus, who had never sinned at all, not only welcomed us, but also took our punishment upon him. He took the initiative; he made the decision; it happened because he determined it would happen. All the things we have done to offend God have been atoned for by Jesus, and all the righteousness we need to have right standing before a holy God has been given us in Jesus—it has all been charged to his account.

And in the same way Paul, in pleading on behalf of Onesimus, wrote to Philemon, "I, Paul, am writing this with my own hand; I will repay it," Jesus, with his own hands nailed to a cross, pled on our behalf, "Father forgive them, they do not know what they are doing." Jesus did all this for the Apostle Paul and Martin Luther, for Philemon and Onesimus, for T. S. Eliot and Arthur Miller, for John Proctor and Abigail Williams, for you and me, for Maj, for everyone. Jesus welcomed us, and while we were still sinners, died for us.

Amen.

GOD IS MERCIFUL
TO SINNERS
Marlo Thomas and the Only Acceptance Letter You'll Ever Need

He also told this parable to some who trusted in themselves that they were righteous and regarded others with contempt: "Two men went up to the temple to pray, one a Pharisee and the other a tax collector. The Pharisee, standing by himself, was praying thus, 'God, I thank you that I am not like other people: thieves, rogues, adulterers, or even like this tax collector. I fast twice a week; I give a tenth of all my income.' But the tax collector, standing far off, would not even look up to heaven, but was beating his breast and saying, 'God, be merciful to me, a sinner!' I tell you, this man went down to his home justified rather than the other; for all who exalt themselves will be humbled, but all who humble themselves will be exalted" (Luke 18:9-14).

In the Name of the Father, Son, and Holy Spirit.

Cate, my oldest daughter, recently e-mailed me a link to a hilarious website, "Book-A-Minute," in which there are ultra-condensed versions of many classic books. For Hemingway's *The Old Man and the Sea:* "An old man catches a fish that's too big for his boat. The fish gets eaten by sharks. Then he goes home and dies. The end." Similarly, the collected works of Jane Austin are summarized: "Female Lead: *'I secretly love Male Lead... he must never know.'* Male Lead: *'I secretly love Female Lead... she must never know.'* They find out. The end."

In today's passage from Luke Jesus tells a parable about two kinds of people: those who trust in their own works and those who trust in God's mercy. The "Book-A-Minute" summary of this parable is this: God is merciful to sinners.

Luke emphasizes that Jesus had a specific audience in mind, that he "told his parable to some who trusted in themselves that they were righteous and regarded others with contempt."

Self-reliance like this is ingrained in us from childhood. When I was in grade school in the mid-seventies we would watch episodes of a TV series called *Free to Be You and Me,* which included cartoons and sketches all about being your own person and trusting in yourself. Various celebrities like Michael Jackson, Dustin Hoffman, Cicely Tyson, and Mel Brooks appeared in this show, and every episode featured Marlo Thomas singing the very catchy theme song, which included these lyrics:

> Every boy in this land grows to be his own man
> In this land, every girl grows to be her own woman

> Take my hand, come with me where the children are
> free
> Come with me, take my hand, and we'll run
> To a land where the river runs free…
> And you and me are free to be you and me

I had that song memorized—I could still sing you the chorus. And it's not only Marlo Thomas, she may have gotten it from Ralph Waldo Emerson, the nineteenth century Transcendentalist, wrote this in his piece, *Self-Reliance*: "Trust thyself: every heart vibrates to that iron string."

Unfortunately, Emerson is right. Every heart indeed vibrates to the iron string of self-reliance. Each of us tends to put our trust in ourselves, and since Jesus directed this parable to those who trust in themselves, we are all implicated.

He also directed this parable to those who regard others with contempt.

When officiating for wedding rehearsals, I'm often amazed at how many judgmental looks I see from people *in* the wedding party, as they watch each person process down the aisle, judging dresses, shoes, weight and gait. All of us have been in situations in which we have felt regarded with contempt, or in which we have regarded others with contempt. All of us in one way or another have experienced both the pride in judging and pain of feeling judged. Again, within Jesus' story, we are implicated.

In his parable there are two men who go to the temple to pray: a Pharisee and a tax collector. Jesus first describes the Pharisee as standing by himself and praying. He starts out his prayer well—"God, I thank you…"— but instead of thanking God for all his blessings he thanks God for what a great person he sees in himself: "God I thank you that I am not like other people; thieves, rogues, adulterers, or even like this tax collector." The Pharisee sees himself as God's gift to the world; he sees himself literally in a class by himself. He takes pride not only in what he does—"I fast twice a week; I give a tenth of all my income"— but also in what he chooses *not* to do, like steal or commit adultery.

The Pharisee is dripping with self-reliance. He prides himself not only for keeping the Old Testament law, but going beyond it. The Pharisee feels as though he has earned enough points to be righteous in the eyes of God.

Of course, this preoccupation with earning enough points is in all of us. Walter Kirn's humorous and poignant memoir, *Lost in the Meritocracy*, says it best, recounting his never-ending chase for more trophies in his life. Kirn writes:

> My SAT scores launched a new phase in a trajectory that I'd been riding since age five... A natural child of the meritocracy I'd been amassing momentum my whole life, entering spelling bees, vying for prizes, plaques, citations, stars, and I gave no thought to any goal beyond my next appearance on the honor roll. Learning was secondary, promotion was primary. No one ever told me what the point was, except to keep on accumulating points, and this struck me as sufficient. What else was there? (9).

Eventually Kirn's incessant need for point growth led to a breakdown, but even after his breakdown, he reverted to the chase. He describes the anxiety of a dead end as he neared graduation:

> I scanned the horizon for another test to take, another contest to compete in. I hadn't learned any lessons from my breakdown. The curse had me right back in its grip. Here I was, just this side of mental paralysis, and again I was starving for medals, stars,

acceptance letters. To me, wealth and power were trivial by-products of improving one's statistical scores in the great generational tournament of aptitude. The ranking itself was the essential prize (189).

The tax collector is the other man in the parable. Hated for working for the Romans, tax collectors in Jesus' day had the authority both to appraise something and then decide how much tax needed to be paid for it. They had booths, similar to toll booths, along the road and would collect taxes from farmers and merchants heading in and out of town. There were often Roman soldiers who accompanied the tax collectors to make sure the taxes were paid. Fraud ran rampant, and while tax collectors tended to be extremely wealthy they were often extremely hated as well, especially by the pious Pharisees.

But unlike the Pharisee, the tax collector is marked by humility. Jesus tells us that "the tax collector, standing far off, would not even look up to heaven, but was beating his breast and saying, 'God be merciful to me, a sinner.'"

The humility of the tax collector was evident in both his posture and his words. The tax collector does not arrogantly prance into the temple and look up to heaven while informing God about what an amazing guy he has been. The tax collector does not recite a litany of all the wonderful things he's done. The tax collector simply appeals to the mercy of God: "God, be merciful to me, a sinner."

In fact, the phrase "a sinner" could be more accurately translated, "*the* sinner." This is not a mere grammatical technicality, but reveals that unlike the Pharisee who thanks God that he is not like other people who were sinners, the tax collector sees himself not only as a sinner, but as *the* sinner. Unlike the Pharisee who considers himself to be in a class by himself as a paragon of righteousness, the tax collector finds himself to be in a class by himself as *the* sinner.

Similarly, the Apostle Paul, who had been a Pharisee and a vehement persecutor of the church, saw himself as the "foremost" of sinners (1 Timothy 1:15).

The good news is that God answers the tax collector's prayer. The good news is that God is merciful to sinners, sinners like the tax collector, sinners like the Apostle Paul, sinners like you and me.

And because God is merciful to sinners, the tax collector "went down to his home justified." To be justified means to be righteous in God's sight, to be accepted by God, to be found innocent. This justification is an entirely free gift of God in Jesus Christ. It is not based on one iota of anything we have done or not done. Justification is not based on how many points we have earned in the meritocracy. It is freely offered to all of us.

This is because, in his death on the cross, Jesus Christ, the Son of God, paid the price for our justification. Regarded with contempt, Jesus Christ became *the* sinner in our place, as Paul wrote to the Corinthians "For our sake He made him to be sin who knew no sin, so that in him we might become the righteousness of God" (2 Corinthians 5:21). Jesus paid the debt we owe God for our sin, every penny, and he didn't do it out of anger; he did it out of love.

And because of Jesus' death on the cross we too, like the tax collector, can go home today justified, assured that we have been forgiven and accepted by God.

All that's left is to believe that justification. Listen to what Cranmer preached about justification by faith:

> This saying, that we be justified by faith only, freely, and without works, is spoken for to take away clearly all merit of our works, as being unable to deserve our justification at God's hands; and thereby most plainly to express the weakness

of man and the goodness of God, the great infirmity of ourselves and the might and power of God, the imperfectness of our own works and the most abundant grace of our Savior Christ; and thereby wholly for to ascribe the merit and deserving of our justification unto Christ only.

Cranmer makes it crystal clear that justification, acceptance with God, is based solely on trusting in God's mercy, not our works.

A couple years ago I was emailed a video of a dad who had a son who suffered with cerebral palsy, whose arms and legs were curled up at his sides all the time. The dad adored his son, and he also competed in Ironman triathlons. The video montage showed the dad gently placing his son in a raft and then pulling him as he swam 2.4 miles, then placing his son in a custom-built bike seat for the 112-mile bike ride, then placing his son in a stroller for the 26.2-mile marathon. At the finish line there was not a dry eye, the dad and his son were laughing and hugging. The son was completely dependent on his dad, and his dad loved him and got him all the way to the finish line. That's what the mercy of God is like.

The truth is that although trusting in ourselves is something that we're brought up believing, eventually the iron string of self-reliance rings hollow, eventually all of us find ourselves like the tax collector—head down, standing at arm's length, feeling like *the* sinner, desperately in need of the mercy of God.

The good news is that God is merciful to sinners. The good news is that like the tax collector we can put our trust in a merciful God. The good news is that the death of Jesus on the cross is proof once and for all that, as we pray each week in the prayer of humble access, we serve a God "whose property is always to have mercy" (BCP, 337).

Amen.

A CHANCE TO LIVE AGAIN

The Clarence Effect and the Power of Repentance

In those days John the Baptist appeared in the wilderness of Judea, proclaiming, "Repent, for the kingdom of heaven has come near" (Matthew 3:1-2).

In the Name of the Father, Son, and the Holy Spirit.

Every year in December I watch my all-time favorite movie, *It's a Wonderful Life,* the classic 1946 film starring Jimmy Stewart, who plays the part of George Bailey. George is burdened with the task of sustaining a struggling building and loan company. At one point in the film one of the employees loses a huge sum of money and George is threatened with going to prison and losing everything—his job, his family, his reputation. Having been told he was worth more dead than alive because of his life insurance policy, George stands on a bridge and is considering killing himself when his guardian angel, Clarence, jumps in the river. After George rescues Clarence from the river, Clarence gives him a glimpse of what the world would be like without him. Near the end of the film George is completely undone and returns to the bridge and cries out to God: "I want to live again. I want to live again. Please God, let me live again."

In the Gospel lesson for today, the Second Sunday of Advent, we see many people who, like George Bailey are burdened and looking for the chance to live again. John the Baptist had begun preaching a very simple message in the wilderness of Judea: "Repent, for the kingdom of heaven has come near." Many people from Jerusalem and Judea were heading out into the wilderness to confess their sins and be baptized by John in the Jordan River. The burden of their sins was too much for them to bear anymore. They needed relief. They wanted to live again.

And it's not just George Bailey or the people from today's Gospel lesson who are burdened. Everyone is burdened, weighed down in one way or another with something that is just too big. Some wear a burdened expression on their face while others may hide it behind a smile, but everyone is burdened in one way or another. Some are burdened with a sickness that has no cure or debt that appears too massive to ever pay off. Others are burdened with dysfunctional relationships that seem to only be getting even more dysfunctional as time goes by. Still others are burdened with unrelenting stress at work or trying to find a job in the first place. Still others are burdened with self-hatred or addiction or other self-destructive behaviors.

But there is an even greater burden that subsists below all of these, a burden with which everyone struggles, a burden that is too much for anyone to bear: the burden of sin.

And there is only one way for the burden of sin to be relieved, and that is to repent, as John the Baptist preached: "Repent, for the kingdom of heaven has come near."

John the Baptist was the son of Zechariah, a priest, and his wife, Elizabeth. An angel had told Zechariah that his son John would "turn many of the people of Israel to the Lord their God" and "with the spirit and power of Elijah... make ready a people prepared for the Lord" (Luke 1:16-17).

The entire message of all the Old Testament prophets can be summarized in one word: *repent.*

When John the Baptist came onto the scene it had been four centuries since there had been a prophet preaching repentance in Israel. In fact, four hundred years earlier God had spoken through the prophet Malachi that he would send Elijah again to preach repentance, and Jesus identified John the Baptist as fulfilling this prophesy (Malachi 4:5 and Matthew 11:14). Like Elijah in the days of old, John the Baptist lived an austere life in the wilderness, clothed with camel hair and a leather belt, living on a diet of locusts and wild honey. And John preached the same message Elijah preached: repent.

To repent is not just feeling bad about sin or being sorry for it. The biblical scholar D. A. Carson describes repentance as "not a merely intellectual change of mind or mere grief, still less doing penance, but a radical transformation of the entire person, a fundamental turnaround involving mind and action" (*Expositor's Bible Commentary*, Vol. 8, 99).

To repent is to make a u-turn of the entire direction of one's life.

There are two sides to repentance: *turning away* from what is wrong and *turning to* God, as the Apostle Paul wrote to the Thessalonians: "You turned *to* God *from* idols, to serve a living and true God" (1:9).

We see both sides of repentance clearly in the baptism liturgy in *The Book of Common Prayer*. Those being baptized *turn away* from what is wrong by renouncing "Satan and all the spiritual forces of wickedness that rebel against God;" renouncing "the evil powers of this world which corrupt and destroy the creatures of God;" and renouncing "all sinful desires that draw you from the love of God." After renouncing, turning away from, these things, those being baptized *turn to* God, as the celebrant asks, "Do you turn to Jesus Christ and accept him as your Savior... Do you put your whole trust in his grace and love?" (*BCP*, 302).

Repentance is radically urgent. It is not food for thought or consideration for a later time. It is a life and death issue that calls for immediate action. In today's lesson when the Pharisees and Sadducees come to John, the language is urgent: "Even now the ax is lying at the root of the trees; every tree therefore that does not bear good fruit is cut down and thrown into the fire."

We are often bombarded with advertisements urging us to act now, not to put it off another second, but we know that at the end of the day, when it comes to buying things, we don't *have* to act now—that instead it often makes sense to "sleep on it" before making a major purchase—but when it comes to repentance it seems to be a must.

Putting off repentance is always a bad move. Putting off repentance only makes the burden of sin heavier.

I was having lunch with someone once and he was honest with me about the sin in his life. He knew it was wrong but he did not want to repent—"But you know," he said, "it's really wearing me out." Putting off repentance does just that, it wears us out. The burden of sin just gets heavier and heavier. Like Lady Macbeth in Shakespeare's classic play, *Macbeth*, when we try to cover up the sins in our lives, the burden just gets heavier and heavier and in time it can literally drive us to the breaking point.

In T. S. Eliot's *The Cocktail Party*, one of the main characters, Edward, is listening to one of the guests at the cocktail party, Henry, who is describing the fragile state of Edward's marriage to his wife Lavinia: "You made a decision," Henry tells Edward, "You set in motion forces in your life and in the lives of others which cannot be reversed."

A number of years ago I took a few dozen high school students on a ski trip. One of the students was Chris, a huge kid who played on the offensive line of his football team. His nickname was "Freight Train." The problem was, while Chris was a great football player, he was a hapless skier. Late one afternoon I watched in horror as Chris was flying down the slope, screaming. After mowing down a good number of beginners, at the bottom of the slope he wiped out, skidding into another group of skiers standing in a lift line, knocking them down like bowling pins. How indicative is that of life in general? When we find ourselves flying downhill and we run the risk of not only hurting others on the way down, but experiencing a catastrophic wipeout at the end?

Repentance, *turning away from* sin and *turning to God*, is not a one-time event in our lives. While there may be an initial repentance when we first hear the Gospel or receive Christ, we don't stop sinning. Like the nineteenth-century humorist Josh Billings, a contemporary of Mark Twain, once wrote: "It is much easier to repent of sins that we have committed than to repent of those we intend to commit." It's like the Apostle Paul says, "For I know that nothing good dwells within me, that is, in my flesh. I can will what is right, but I cannot do it. For I do not do the good I want, but the evil I do not want is what I do" (Romans 7:18-19).

So what do we do? We repent... and we repent again... and we keep on repenting. We keep turning away from the world, the flesh, and the devil and turning back to God. We keep turning away from sin and turning back to God, for the good news of the Gospel is that "There is therefore now no condemnation for those who are in Christ Jesus" (Romans 8:1).

One of the most important parts of our worship each week is the confession, which is all about repentance. In the Rite One confession we see that repentance brings relief from the burden of sin, as we pray: "We do earnestly repent and are heartily sorry for these our misdoings; the remembrance of them is grievous unto us, the burden of them is intolerable" *(BCP, 331)*.

And what happens when we confess our sins to God? What happens when we repent? God forgives us and takes the burden of sin away. Scripture tells us, "If we confess our sins, he who is faithful and just will forgive us our sins and cleanse us from all unrighteousness" (1 John 1:9). Repentance brings relief.

But this repentance is not something we do in and of ourselves. We repent in response to the love of God by the power of the Holy Spirit.

Rather than repenting to earn God's love, we repent in response to it, for scripture tells us that it is the kindness of God that *leads* us to repentance (Romans 2:4). For one of those who came to the wilderness to be baptized by John was none other than Jesus Christ, whom John identified as the Lamb of God who takes away the sin of the world.

In fact, Jesus actually preached the exact same message as John: "Repent and believe the good news" (Mark 1:15). But Jesus did much more than preach repentance, he took the judgment for our sins upon himself. He took the damage that our sin does to us upon himself. He took the damage that our sin does to others upon himself. Metaphorically the ax was laid to the root of his tree, the cross, and he died in our place.

Scripture tells us that we are fully known and fully loved by God, that while we were still sinners Christ died for us, that

Jesus came into the world not condemn us but to save us, that nothing can separate us from the love of God (Romans 5:8; John 3:17; and Romans 8:39).

Our repentance is in response to the love of God in Jesus Christ. In his classic devotional, *My Utmost for His Highest*, Oswald Chambers describes this:

> It is not repentance that saves me; repentance is the sign that I realize what God has done in Christ Jesus... Is it my obedience that puts me right with God? Never! I am put right with God because prior to all else, Christ died. When I turn to God and by belief accept what God reveals, instantly the stupendous atonement of Jesus Christ rushes me into a right relationship with God. By the miracle of God's grace I stand justified, not because of anything I have done, but because of what Jesus has done (October 28).

Moreover, it is the Holy Spirit who opens our hearts to the love of God. It is the Holy Spirit who enables us to repent, for "no one can say 'Jesus is Lord' except by the Holy Spirit" (I Corinthians 12:3), and "it is God who is at work in (us), enabling (us) both to will and to work for his good pleasure" (Philippians 2:13). It is the Holy Spirit who works in our hearts to urge us to repent, to turn away from sin and turn to God, to experience relief from the burden of sin.

So if today you are feeling the burden of sin in your life, perhaps the Holy Spirit is moving your heart to do the only thing that will bring relief: repent.

Let's return for just a moment to the film, *It's a Wonderful Life*. Remember the prayer George Bailey prays on the bridge? "I want to live again. I want to live again. Please God, let me live again." God answered that prayer, but it gets better. George arrives home just moments before his home is flooded with people from the community who all pitch in money to bail him out of trouble. George doesn't contribute a cent; it was all covered freely and willfully by his friends and neighbors, simply because they loved him and wanted to take his burden away.

And that is exactly what Jesus does for us. He died on the cross to take our burden of sin away, freely and willfully. In response to the downhill velocity of our sin-sickness Jesus ascended the hill of Calvary and through his death set in motion a force in our lives that can never be reversed, the forgiveness of God. Where sin abounds, the grace of God abounds more (Romans 5:20). When we repent, God gives us relief from the burden of sin, because he bore that burden on Calvary.

Amen.

GOD IS FAITHFUL
Love from the Roller Rink

God is faithful; by him you were called into the fellowship of his Son, Jesus Christ our Lord (1 Corinthians 1:9).

In the Name of the Father, Son, and the Holy Spirit.

In the mid-90s my family and I lived in Wyoming for a year, during which we visited Yellowstone National Park. One of our favorite sites was the famous geyser Old Faithful. Old Faithful was given its name during an expedition in 1870 and remains one of the most famous attractions of Yellowstone. Every hour or two Old Faithful erupts and shoots roughly 4-8,000 gallons of boiling water anywhere from 100 to 185 feet high. When we visited, we stood around with a few hundred other tourists waiting for the eruption. Our daughters, Cate and Becky, who were 4 and 3 respectively, became quite restless as we waited, but when Old Faithful erupted, as everyone knew it would, all of us cheered. It is truly an amazing sight.

In today's passage from 1 Corinthians we read the concise but loaded phrase, "God is faithful." To be faithful means to be found reliable. Faithfulness is determined loyalty.

Several years ago my wife bought a sign for the mantel above the fireplace in our family room. It simply says, "God is faithful." And every day when I walk in that room or in the middle of the night if I'm having trouble sleeping and go in there to read, I see that sign and am reminded that no matter what, God is faithful.

This is good to know, because while God is faithful, we are not. People are fickle. In the Old Testament the writer of Proverbs asks, "A faithful man who can find?" (20:6). It's a rhetorical question—the answer for which is a resounding "No one." Moreover, the writer of Proverbs also observes, "Like a bad tooth or a lame foot is trust in a faithless person in times of trouble" (25:19). In times of trouble, we need friends we can count on.

A faithful friend in times of trouble is one of the greatest blessings in life. Think about it: if you were in trouble, or faced with that massive 3 a.m. life crisis, who would you call? Would you have anyone to call? As you look back on your life in those times, who was there for you? Who stood by you? Those are the faithful friends, and if we're honest, friends of that caliber tend to be very few and far between.

Regardless of our idiosyncrasies and weaknesses, faithful friends give us the benefit of the doubt. Faithful friends know nearly everything about us and, oddly enough, like us anyway. Faithful friends are there to give us grace.

While faithful friends tend to be few in number, "frenemies" tend to be common. My middle school daughters introduced me to the concept of "frenemies," when describing the fickle behavior of their classmates and neighbors who go from being their best friend to their worst enemy within a day or two. A "frenemy" is a combination of friend and enemy. I read an article in *Business Week* that describes a "frenemy" as:

> a person you spend time with, enjoy talking with, and rely on at work—but you can't completely trust. He or she is so much a part of your working day that a relationship that isn't strictly business between you is not just assumed—it's unavoidable. And, day in and day out, it's not unpleasant. But at the same time you have been burned by this person, who hasn't demonstrated the unyielding loyalty and support you'd expect—and get— from an out-and-out friend.

Unfortunately the "frenemy" concept is not restricted to school or the office. "Frenemies" abound in neighborhoods, fraternities and sororities, sports teams. Sometimes there are "frenemies" in churches and families. Any organization or institution, any group of people who are together frequently will likely have at least some degree of "frenemy" behavior. As the author of the *Business Week* article put it, we need to be aware of the "Frenemy at the Gates."

"Frenemies" make life stressful. At the end of the day "frenemies" cannot be counted on because "frenemies" are fickle.

One of my favorite rock bands is Journey, a band out of San Francisco whose popularity peaked in the late 70s and early 80s. In middle school, when I'd routinely go roller skating, every hour or so the lights would dim except for a few lights shining on the ever-rotating disco ball, and the DJ would announce in a deep soulful, Don Cornelius wannabe voice, "This is a couples-only skate... couples only... time to take the hand of that special someone and get out on that floor." And it seemed like almost every time there was a couples-only skate, the DJ played one of Journey's power ballads: "Open Arms" or "Still They Ride" or the best one of all, "Faithfully" (from the classic 1983 album, *Frontiers*). I still remember stumbling through a couples-only skate with sweaty palms, nervously skating with a beautiful girl, trying to be cool, envious of those who skated better than me, all the while Steve Perry, Journey's lead singer, wailing, "I'm forever yours, forever yours... faithfully."

We all want to be loved in that way—we long to be loved forever, and faithfully—and we all want to be able to express that kind of forever, faithful love to someone else. But eventually we all fail at this. The bad news is that we are all, despite those efforts, the fickle "frenemies" to others, even the ones we love.

But the good news of the Gospel is that Jesus is *not* our "frenemy." Jesus is the faithful friend of sinners (Matthew 11:19). The good news of the Gospel is that, although people are fickle, God is faithful.

We see this over and over again in Scripture. In spite of the fickleness of people, God remains faithful. After Adam and Eve sinned, God immediately promised he would send a savior in the future (Genesis 3:15). In spite of all the times Israel turned their backs on God and wallowed in idolatry and immorality, God remained faithful and kept the covenant he had made with Israel, as he stated in Deuteronomy, "the Lord your God is God, the faithful God who maintains covenant loyalty" (Deuteronomy 7:9).

There is no limit to the faithfulness of God, as the Psalmist proclaims, "Your love, O Lord, reaches to the heavens, and your faithfulness to the clouds" (Psalm 36:5). Even in the midst of Israel's darkest hour, when the Babylonians conquered Judah and destroyed Jerusalem, the prophet Jeremiah cried out to God, "Great is your faithfulness" (Lamentations 3:23).

And we see that "God is faithful" in our lesson from 1 Corinthians 1:9. Paul founded the Christian church at Corinth during his second missionary journey (Acts 18:1-17). Corinth was a prosperous, cosmopolitan Greek city and the Christian church there grew rapidly. But the church at Corinth was riddled with problems: partisanship, confusion about worship, sexual immorality, members taking one another to court, and doubt about the resurrection. The Corinthian church was filled with problems because it was made up of people who, like you and me, are fickle. But while people are fickle, God is faithful.

There are two times in 1 Corinthians that Paul states, "God is faithful." The first time is in today's passage in which Paul emphasizes that the same God who called us to begin with will remain faithful to us no matter what:

> (God) will also strengthen you to the end, so that you may be blameless on the day of our Lord Jesus Christ. God is faithful; by him you were called into the fellowship of his Son, Jesus Christ our Lord (1:8-9).

In other words, it was not your idea or my idea to be a Christian; we responded to the call of God who spoke to our hearts by the Holy Spirit, the same Holy Spirit who called to the Apostle Paul, the same Holy Spirit who called to the Christians in Corinth. And God is faithful to his call. God always finishes what he starts, and that includes the work he has begun in our lives, as Paul encouraged the Philippians: "I am confident of this, that the one who began a good work among you will bring it to completion by the day of Jesus Christ" (Philippians 1:6).

The other time Paul states, "God is faithful" in 1 Corinthians is when discussing the reality of temptation:

> No temptation has seized you except what is common to man. And God is faithful: he will

not let you be tempted beyond what you can bear. But when you are tempted, he will also provide a way out so that you can stand up under it (1 Corinthians 10:13, NIV).

In other words, when we *are* tempted, we can be encouraged because God is faithful—he always provides an exit sign. The problem is even when we see the exit sign in the midst of temptation, sometimes we ignore it. When I think about times I have sinned in my life I can look back and remember that there was indeed an exit sign, there was a way out of that temptation, but I didn't take it. I sinned anyway, because I'm fickle. Perhaps you can relate.

So while the bad news is that we are fickle, the good news is God is faithful—in 1 Corinthians we see that God is faithful to us no matter what and that God is faithful to us during temptation. Incidentally, several decades after Paul was martyred one of the early church fathers, Clement of Rome, also wrote a Letter to the Christians at Corinth. He addressed some of the exact same issues that Paul had addressed decades earlier in his letters, but while the Christians at Corinth remained fickle, God remained faithful.

The ultimate demonstration of God's faithfulness is found in Jesus Christ. God kept the promise he made to Adam and Eve in the garden. God kept the covenant he made with Israel, and sent a Savior, Jesus Christ. Jesus Christ the faithful Friend of sinners, died on the cross to forgive us for all the times we have been fickle, to forgive us for all the times we have seen the exit sign in the midst of temptation and ignored it, to forgive us for all the times we have acted as "frenemies" towards others.

In fact, at the Last Supper Jesus called his disciples, "friends" and told them there was no greater love than for someone to lay down his life for his friends (John 15:13-14), and even though within hours they would all run away as his suffering began, Jesus was a faithful friend and still gave the greatest demonstration of love ever. In spite of the fickleness of the disciples, and the fickleness of you and me, Jesus, the "faithful high priest" (Hebrews 2:17), gave his life for all of us.

Infinitely more magnificent than the fountain of Old Faithful at Yellowstone is the fountain of mercy and grace that flowed from Jesus on the cross, as the English hymnist William Cowper beautifully put it:

> There is a fountain filled with blood
> Drawn from Emmanuel's veins;
> And sinners, plunged beneath that flood,
> Lose all their guilty stains.

And scripture makes it very clear that when we confess to God that we are fickle sinners, "(God) *who is faithful* and just will forgive us our sins and cleanse us from all unrighteousness" (1 John 1:9). This is possible because God is faithful and sent Jesus to save us, just as he promised.

And right now, this very moment, regardless of how fickle you and I may be, we can be encouraged and comforted because God is faithful, no matter what, that as Paul wrote to his protégé Timothy: "If we are faithless, (God) remains faithful—for he cannot deny himself" (2 Timothy 2:13).

And just as Jesus promised after his resurrection, we know that one day he will return to complete his great work of salvation. In the last book of the Bible, Revelation, John records a vision of the return of Jesus. Listen to how John refers to Jesus the returning king: "Then I saw heaven opened, and there was a white horse! Its rider is called *Faithful* and True" (Revelation 19:11). Jesus, the faithful High Priest, the faithful Friend of Sinners, the rider called Faithful, will return and complete his great work of salvation, and for all eternity we will enjoy the forever faithful love of God.

I'll close with a brief story. In 1866 a boy named Thomas Chisholm was born in a cabin in Franklin, Kentucky. He was converted to Christ at the age of 27 and briefly served as a Methodist minister but struggled with ill health and burned out. He spent the rest of his life selling insurance in New Jersey. His life had not gone according to plan, but in spite of the unceasing struggles with his health and finances he wrote over 1200 poems, one of which was put to music and became one of the best-loved hymns ever: *Great is Thy Faithfulness*. The first verse and refrain say it all:

> Great is Thy faithfulness, O God my Father.
> There is no shadow of turning with Thee.
> Thou changest not, Thy compassions, they fail not.
> As Thou hast been, Thou forever will be.
>
> Great is Thy faithfulness!
> Great is Thy faithfulness!
> Morning by morning new mercies I see.
> All I have needed Thy hand hath provided.
> Great is Thy faithfulness, Lord, unto me!

Even though we are fickle, God is faithful, no matter what. It is much more than a sign that can be placed on a mantel; it is the good news of the Gospel that the Holy Spirit can place in your heart.

Amen.

THE ELEVATOR
DOOR IS ALWAYS
OPEN
Old Wounds and God's Reconciling Love

> *So when you are offering your gift at the altar, if you remember that your brother or sister has something against you, leave your gift there before the altar and go; first be reconciled to your brother or sister, and then come and offer your gift (Matthew 5:23-24).*

In the Name of the Father, Son, and Holy Spirit.

In the multiple Oscar-winning 1979 film, *Kramer vs. Kramer,* Meryl Streep and Dustin Hofmann, portray a couple, Ted and Joanna Kramer, whose marriage ends in divorce and a bitter custody battle over their son, Billy. The film includes a recurring metaphor of a closing elevator door.

Near the beginning of the film Joanna leaves Ted, and while she is on an elevator he begs her not to go, to which she replies, "I don't love you anymore," and the door closes. Later in the film after a brutal day in court as Ted boards an elevator Joanna tries to apologize to him for her lawyer raking him over the coals during the custody hearings—he looks at her and says nothing as the door closes. Although Joanna wins the custody battle she decides Billy would be better off with Ted, and in the final scene of the film Joanna boards an elevator as she goes to tell Billy goodbye. She has been crying, and her make-up is running, and she asks Ted, "How do I look?" Ted smiles and replies, "Terrific." The elevator door closes and the credits roll. The film never shows Ted and Joanna riding the elevator together. There is no reconciliation.

The film *Kramer vs. Kramer* resonates because it rings true to our experience. Sometimes in our lives relationships lack reconciliation, and this lack of reconciliation can create feelings that ricochet between hidden resentment and open hostility. It's not the way it's supposed to be but it's the way it is. We live in a world in which marriages sometimes end in divorce, grown children sometimes refuse to have anything to do with their parents, and best friends become estranged. This lack of reconciliation can feel like a burden or a dark cloud hanging overhead.

In today's passage from the Sermon on the Mount Jesus speaks right to this: "When you are offering your gift at the altar, if you remember that your brother or sister has something against you, leave your gift there before the altar and go; first be reconciled to your brother or sister, and then come and offer your gift" (Matthew 5:23-24).

Reconciliation matters to God.

A few weeks ago I was pulling up to a stoplight and in front of me was a large pick-up truck with a bumper sticker with "Jesus" in large letters followed by something else. I inched closer and saw that it said, "JESUS loves you but everyone else thinks you're a jerk." Scripture tells us that God loves us all the time, even when we're jerks, and the truth is all of us act like a jerk to other people sometimes. But although this is true, it doesn't make it *right*, and it is not the best for our lives. Jesus makes it clear that if we remember that someone has something against us that we are to go to them and try to be reconciled. Apparently Jesus considers reconciliation more important than worship: "leave your gift there at the altar and go," he says, "first be reconciled to your brother or sister, and then come and offer your gift."

Our reconciliation with others is in response to *being* reconciled to God through the death of Jesus on the cross. As Paul wrote in his Second Letter to the Corinthians, "(God has) reconciled us to himself through Christ, and has given us the ministry of reconciliation" (5:18); and as the Anglican scholar Michael Green puts in *The Message of Matthew*: "Reconciliation with others flows from reconciliation with God" (94).

The good news of the Gospel is that we have been reconciled to God, and therefore can be reconciled with others. Reconciliation with God is a recurring theme in the letters of the Apostle Paul. In Romans we read: "For if while we were enemies, we were reconciled to God through the death of his Son, much more surely, having been reconciled, will we be saved by his life... we have now received reconciliation" (Romans 5:10-11).

In fact, in the fifth chapter of Romans Paul emphasizes that reconciliation with God is something that is done *for* us rather than something we do ourselves. In other words, we don't reconcile ourselves to God—we cannot—but God reconciles us to himself through the death of Jesus on the cross. This reconciliation is a gift we receive through faith, through trust in Jesus Christ.

Moreover, Paul stresses that God took the initiative to reconcile us to himself when it was the last thing on our minds, when the elevator doors were closing and we did not want them open again. Paul tells us "while we were still weak" Jesus died for us, "while we were still sinners" Jesus died for us, "while we were enemies" Jesus died for us.

In his book, *The Apostolic Preaching of the Cross*, Leon Morris describes how Jesus' death on the cross gives us complete reconciliation with God:

> No true reconciliation can take place unless the cause of the estrangement is truly faced and dealt with. If it is ignored or glossed over, then a species of uneasy truce may result, but there can be no real restoration of fellowship, no true reconciliation... But in the death of Him whom God 'made sin' for man the cause of the enmity was squarely faced and removed. Therefore a complete reconciliation results, so that man turns to God in repentance and trust, and God looks on man with favor and not in wrath (249).

In other words, the good news of the Gospel is that when it comes to being reconciled with God, the elevator door stays open. That means reconciliation with others is possible, that we can leave our gift at the altar and first be reconciled with those who have something against us and then worship God. "Reconciliation with others flows from reconciliation with God."

We see this in the Holy Communion service. First we confess our sins to God and receive anew his forgiveness, then we pass the peace with others, and after that we give our gifts to God and receive communion.

What does it look like to be reconciled with others? It's important to remember that Jesus said, "be reconciled to your brother or sister," *not* "reconcile your brother and sister to you." Many years ago I heard a preacher suggest the following three sentences for seeking to be reconciled with others: "I'm sorry. I was wrong. Please forgive me." (When it comes to reconciliation with others this tends to be more helpful than: "I'm not sorry. You're an idiot. Get out of my life.")

"I'm sorry. I was wrong. Please forgive me"—no excuses, no disclaimers, no passing the buck, no blaming extenuating circumstances or lack of sleep or the weather, no self-justifying "I really didn't mean it" or "I'm just really stressed right now"—just a humble, simple, straight-up apology.

"I'm sorry. I was wrong. Please forgive me"—we can say these things to those with whom we wish to be reconciled because we have been reconciled to God. While Jesus had nothing to be sorry for, he paid the penalty for our sins anyway; while Jesus did nothing wrong, he died for our wrongs anyway; and while Jesus had nothing to ask forgiveness for, he died for us anyway so that we could be forgiven. "Father forgive them," he prayed as he was nailed to the cross, "for they do not know what they are doing."

But like so many things, apologizing to others is easier said than done. The truth is our apologies are often riddled with excuses and disclaimers, and we often misread those who have something against us. In his moving 1997 Pulitzer-Prize winning novel *American Pastoral*, Philip Roth describes how sometimes we are simply *wrong* about others:

> You fight your superficiality, your shallowness, so as to try to come at people without unreal expectations, without an overload of bias or hope or arrogance, as untanklike as you can be, sans cannon and machine guns and steel plating half a foot

thick… and yet you never fail to get them wrong. You might as well have the *brain* of a tank. You get them wrong before you meet them, while you're anticipating meeting them; you get them wrong while you're with them; and then you go home and tell someone else about the meeting and you get them all wrong again… The fact remains that getting people right is not what living is all about anyway. It's getting them wrong that is living, getting them wrong and wrong and wrong and then, on careful reconsideration, getting them wrong again. That's how we know we're alive; we're wrong. Maybe the best thing would be to forget being right or wrong about people and just go along for the ride. But if you can do that—well, lucky you (*35*).

In observing that we are often wrong about others, Roth gets it exactly right. We need the grace of God, especially when it comes to being reconciled with others.

In human relationships, sometimes we apologize and are forgiven. We are reconciled to that person—the burden is lifted, the black cloud is no longer hanging overhead.

When I was in grade school there was a kid in my grade named Sean. In 2nd, 3rd, and 4th grades we were not in the same class but often competed and argued at P.E. and recess. We were fierce rivals and couldn't stand each other. On the first day of 5th grade, to our dismay, we found ourselves in the same class. Things regressed and a couple weeks later we got in a fistfight at recess. We were sent to the office, lips swollen and faces bruised. While awaiting our doom at the hands of the assistant principle we apologized to each other and were reconciled. From then on we were best friends, and spent many hours playing basketball after school with Van Halen blaring from a boom box. Life was good.

Sometimes reconciliation happens after many years, when those involved thought it would most likely never happen. One of the most moving stories in the Old Testament is that of Joseph and his reconciliation with his brothers (Genesis 43-45). Joseph was the favorite of Jacob's twelve sons, evident by Jacob's gift of a coat of many colors. Out of jealousy Joseph's brothers sold him into slavery, and then dipped his coat into animal blood so that it would look like he had been slain by a wild animal. Then they gave the bloody coat to their father.

Joseph's brothers watched their father Jacob suffer from grief, and not a single one of them ever confessed it to Jacob. God preserved and prospered Joseph, who eventually became second only to Pharaoh over all Egypt. Seeking relief from extreme famine Jacob's brothers eventually went to Egypt for food and were later reconciled with Joseph.

Guess how long it was between Joseph's being sold into slavery by his brothers and their reconciliation? *Twenty years*—talk about family dysfunction! I imagine neither Joseph nor his brothers ever thought they would see each other again, let alone be reconciled, but God's grace made it possible, in time.

But unfortunately when we try to be reconciled with others it doesn't always end like it did with me and Sean or Joseph and his brothers. Sometimes when we apologize we are not forgiven, there is no reconciliation, and the black cloud remains. Some people simply enjoy nursing grudges. Some people would rather keep the elevator door closed.

But there is grace in this case as well, for Scripture tells us, "If it is possible, so much as it depends on you, live peaceably with all" (Romans 12:18). In other words, by God's grace we can keep the elevator door open for those with whom we wish to be reconciled, and God will work that out in his time. Scripture tells us that "in (Jesus) all the fullness of God was pleased to dwell, and through him God was pleased to reconcile to himself all things, whether on earth or in heaven, by making peace through the blood of his cross" (Colossians 1:19-20). We can be assured that because of the death of Jesus on the cross not only have we been reconciled to God, we can rest in the hope that someday God will reconcile all things in our lives, including bringing reconciliation with those with whom we wish to be reconciled.

What about you today? Perhaps there are people in your life with whom God is calling you to be reconciled, or perhaps you've already tried to be reconciled but reconciliation won't occur. The good news is that, in Jesus' death on the cross, you have already *been* reconciled to God, fully. The burden has been lifted, the black cloud has vanished.

By God's grace you have been reconciled to him, by God's grace you can be reconciled with others, and by God's grace you can be assured that one day everything will be reconciled once and for all.

The good news of the Gospel is that by God's grace the elevator door is always open.

Amen.

WHY HAVE YOU FORSAKEN ME?

"Cowper's Grave" and the Shared Loneliness of God

"My God, my God, why have you forsaken me?"
(Matthew 27:46).

In the Name of the Father, Son, and Holy Spirit.

Normally I try to include humor and levity when I preach, but that will not be the case today. This is a rather dark sermon.

I'm preaching on just one aspect of Jesus' passion and death: his cry of dereliction from the cross—*"My God, my God, why have you forsaken me?"* This cry is the only statement of Jesus from the cross recorded by Matthew (27:46).

To be forsaken means to be deserted or disowned. Most of us can recount episodes in our lives when we were forsaken.

Some endure the pain of being forsaken by a parent when a little child. I recently read an article in *The New York Times* about a married couple in China on a train with their daughter who looked to be about four or five years old. At one of the stations the three of them stepped off the train. The couple asked the little girl to have a seat on the bench for awhile, and then boarded the train again and left their little girl sitting on the bench alone. They never came back for her.

Some endure the heartbreak of being forsaken or dumped by a boyfriend or girlfriend in school. I still remember being on the dance floor at a homecoming dance in high school when I turned around to see my date slow-dancing with someone else that apparently she liked better. I still remember the hurt and embarrassment I felt on the long and humiliating walk across the dance floor and out of the gym.

Some endure being forsaken by their employer after investing many of the prime years of their lives in a company or firm. This has especially been the case during the turbulent economy of the past few years.

Some are forsaken by their fiancé or spouse. When I was a freshman in college I remember my English professor describing how it felt when she was stood up at the altar on her wedding day, how it felt to be forsaken by her fiancé in front of all her family and friends, how her highly anticipated joyous wedding day became her worst nightmare. Just this past week a friend of our family was notified by her husband of twenty-five years that he is divorcing her, and she and their kids are utterly devastated.

Some parents are forsaken by their grown children and may spend many years if not the rest of their lives with little or no contact with them, each birthday and holiday accompanied by yet another hearty dose of grief.

Most of us have personally experienced the pain of being forsaken. It hurts to the core. The passing of time does not heal it. People who have been forsaken do their best to move forward but often have an emotional limp that never goes away.

And not only can each of us probably recount times in our lives when we were forsaken, we can also recount times when we have done the forsaking, when we have been the one who abandoned, deserted, left behind, disowned someone else. Most of us in one way or another have been on both sides of the equation.

Being forsaken is not only an experience common to us; it was common to Jesus too, particularly in his darkest hours, the hours of his passion. Jesus is forsaken by *everyone*, even his disciples. After Jesus' betrayal and arrest, Matthew tells us, *"all* the disciples *forsook* him and fled" (Matthew 26:56).

After Jesus is arrested he is kept up all night—tried by the high priests, sentenced to death for the false charge of blasphemy, spit on, mocked, and handed over to Roman soldiers. He is questioned by Pilate, hears hundreds of people yell, "Crucify him! Crucify him!" He is beaten, flogged, forced to carry the instrument of his own death to the site of his own death.

By the time Jesus cries out in dereliction he has been hanging on the cross for hours, enduring unspeakable suffering—naked, beaten, bloodied, extreme fatigue and stress causing the muscles throughout his body to cramp and spasm, exposed to the elements and insects, subject to the insults of religious leaders who would not let up, hearing the sneering comments of passersby as he slowly suffocated to death.

Although it is mid-afternoon, darkness has covered the sky and, in this moment, the darkest moment in the history of the universe, Jesus cries out in a loud voice, "My God, my God, why have you forsaken me?"

Interestingly enough, this is the only time in Synoptic Gospels that Jesus is recorded as addressing God as "God" and not "Father." Jesus has even been forsaken by God. He has been abandoned, deserted, left behind, disowned... even by God.

God the Father is fully able to completely stop Jesus' horrific suffering, but God does not. As Jesus suffers on the cross, God is silent.

The late biblical scholar Raymond Brown describes this in *The Death of the Messiah*:

> Jesus has been abandoned by his disciples and mocked by all who have come to the cross. Darkness has covered the earth; there is nothing that shows God acting on Jesus' side... His 'Why?' is that of someone who has plumbed the depths of the abyss, and feels enveloped by the power of darkness. Jesus is not questioning the existence of God or the power of God to do something about what is happening; he is questioning the silence of the one whom he calls 'My God' (1046).

Often when people suffer they ask, "*Why*, God?" "*Why* is this happening?" "*Why* won't you help me?" "*Why* are you silent?" *Why*...?

I've heard it preached before that when we suffer we shouldn't ask, "Why?" but rather "What?" or "How?"— "*What* is God trying to *teach* me?" or "*How* is God *growing* my faith?" That is not the least bit helpful. It's a shoddy attempt to try to find something to control and understand as we suffer, because suffering robs us of our (perceived) ability to control or understand. Jesus did not ask or "what" or "how" questions from the cross. Apparently Jesus, quoting Psalm 22, deemed it appropriate to ask, "Why?" And not just in his heart, but in a loud voice for all around to hear.

In her poem, "Cowper's Grave," the Victorian poet Elizabeth Barrett Browning poignantly describes this moment:

> Deserted! who hath dreamt that when the cross in
> darkness rested
> Upon the Victim's hidden face no love was
> manifested!
> What frantic hands outstretched have e'er the
> atoning drops averted!
> What tears have washed them from the soul, that one
> should be deserted?
> Deserted! God could separate from his own essence
> rather,
> And Adam's sins have swept between the righteous
> Son and Father;
> Yea, once, Immanuel's orphaned cry his universe hath
> shaken,—
> It went up single, echoless, "My God, I am forsaken!"

Here's the good news. For the times in our lives when we have been forsaken God offers comfort and empathy—God gets it. For the times when we have forsaken others God offers mercy and forgiveness. God offers grace for all of it.

For all of us, for all time, God offers us his grace and presence, especially in the midst of suffering. And while there is hardly a clear answer to the "Why?" we cry out when we suffer, there is an answer to Jesus' cry, "My God, my God, why have you forsaken me?"

The reason God forsook Jesus on the cross was because God would not forsake you.

God declares, in both the Old and New Testaments, "I will never leave you or forsake you" (Deuteronomy 31:6, 8 and Hebrews 13:5).

Even though through your sin you have forsaken God, God has never forsaken you. Even though you may have forsaken others or been forsaken by them, God has never forsaken you.

God loves you too much to ever forsake you, and it was out of his love for you that Jesus, God in Christ, was forsaken in your stead.

This is the good news of the Gospel, that on the cross Jesus was forsaken by God in your place because God has never, and will never, forsake you.

Amen.

ONCE FOR ALL
Derek Jeter's Extra-Innings Birthday Present

For Christ also suffered for sins once for all, the righteous for the unrighteous, in order to bring you to God (1 Peter 3:18).

In the Name of the Father, Son, and Holy Spirit.

I recently took my twelve-year old son Paul to Camden Yards to see the Orioles play the Yankees. We had a total blast. The game went to extra innings—*lots* of extra innings. During the 14th inning we did the 14th inning stretch (not joking) and during our second try at "Take Me Out to the Ball Game," Paul said offhandedly that the game hadn't ended yet because God wanted him to get a foul ball first. About ten minutes later, Paul's favorite player, Derek Jeter, fouled the ball off to where we were sitting along the first base line. All I had to do was dive over some seats to grab it.

The grin on his face as I put the ball in his glove—"Happy Birthday"—was one I'll never forget. The five-hour game ended after 15 innings. One of the cool things about baseball is that there is no clock—the winning team cannot run out the clock to seal the win; time cannot run out for the losing team. The game does not end until either the winning run is scored or the final out made. Hold that thought.

Today I'm preaching from the First Letter of Peter. Near the end of his life Peter wrote this Letter to Christians who lived in Asia Minor and were suffering persecution for their faith in Christ. Peter sought to remind them, even in the midst of that suffering, of God's love for them in Jesus Christ.

In 1 Peter 3:18 Peter powerfully summarizes the Gospel: "For Christ suffered for sins once for all, the righteous for the unrighteous, in order to bring you to God." This entire sermon will focus on that one verse.

Peter begins, "For Christ suffered for sins once for all."

No one needs to tell us that sin is rampant in our lives. In his Letter to the Romans the Apostle Paul asserts that people are "filled with wickedness, evil, covetousness, malice" and "full of envy, murder, strife, deceit, craftiness;" that people can be "gossips, slanderers, God-haters, insolent, haughty, boastful, inventors of evil, rebellious toward parents, foolish, faithless, heartless, ruthless" (Romans 1:29-31).

And it is not just the Apostle Paul. Jesus himself speaks of the sinful nature of the human heart. "For it is from within," He said, "from the human heart, that evil intentions come: adultery, avarice, wickedness, deceit, licentiousness, envy, slander, pride, folly. All these evil things come from within, and they defile a person" (Mark 7:21-23).

Neither Jesus nor Paul minced words when describing the rampant sin in our lives. Our personal experience testifies to the truth of what they said. All of us in one way or another have hurt others by our sin or been hurt by the sin of others. This happens our whole lives through, from bullies on the school playground to elderly parents intentionally leaving out certain children from their wills, and every of station of life in between.

I have spent hours listening to people in my office or on my back porch as they pour out their hearts about the hurts and regrets of their lives—the hurts they have suffered at the hands of others or the regret of the suffering they have caused others or the ongoing struggles with people who continue to hurt them.

One of my all time favorite movies is *Good Will Hunting* (1997), a gritty but powerful film starring Matt Damon who plays Will Hunting, a dayshift worker who is brilliant but gets in trouble with the law and in order to avoid time in prison visits a therapist, Sean Maguire, played by Robin Williams. As a boy, Will Hunting had been severely beaten and abused by one of his foster fathers and in one of the climactic scenes of the film, Sean, referring to these painful experiences from Will's past, repeats the phrase, "It's not your fault" to Will over and over. Eventually Will begins sobbing and healing begins to occur. That scene will wipe you out.

The reality is that all of us in one way or another are guilty of the sins listed by Jesus and Paul, guilty of sins that have hurt other people and ourselves. And on the flipside, all of us, like Will Hunting, have been hurt by the sins of others.

The good news is that Jesus understands, that Jesus the Righteous, died for all those sins, every single one, those we have done and those that have been done to us. "Christ suffered for sins once for all," Peter wrote, "the righteous for the unrighteous." The sins we have done are our fault—it does no good blaming it on others or on circumstances—just as much as the sins that have been done unto us are *not* our fault—it does no good accepting the blame for things that are not our fault. But Jesus the righteous, who was completely faultless, died for all of it. None of our sins were Jesus' fault, but he died for them anyway.

The Bible is clear that when it comes to suffering for sin, Jesus Christ has done that for us, in our place: "Christ suffered for sins once for all." This "once for all" nature of Christ's suffering for sin is a common theme in the Bible, that Christ died for every person who has ever lived and who will ever live, and that his "once for all" death is sufficient to pay the punishment for all of our sins. Nothing we do can add or detract from this "once for all" death on the cross—nothing, nothing, absolutely nothing.

And it is not just Peter who emphasizes the completeness of Jesus' sacrifice for our sins; Paul does so as well in Romans: "The death (Jesus Christ) died, *He died to sin, once for all*" (6:10). The Apostle John does this in his first Letter: "Jesus Christ the righteous... is *the atoning sacrifice for our sins*, and not for ours only but also for *the sins of the whole world*" (2:1-2). The Letter to the Hebrews states: "(Jesus) has appeared *once for all* at the end of the age to remove sin by the sacrifice of himself" (9:26).

Moreover each week we are reminded of the "once for all nature" of Jesus' death on the cross for us in the prayers for Holy Communion. In the Eucharistic Prayer we see that Jesus Christ "made there, by his one oblation of himself once offered, a full, perfect, and sufficient sacrifice, oblation, and satisfaction, for the sins of the whole world" *(BCP, 334)*; or in Rite II—"He stretched out his arms upon the cross, and offered himself... a perfect sacrifice for the whole world" *(BCP, 362)*.

I recently flew to Seattle to spend some time with some friends. While I was at a gate at Dulles International Airport waiting to board the flight to Seattle an attendant announced the priority of the order for boarding the plane. In addition to those with small children or the elderly or infirm there was a complex ranking system for boarding the plane. Customers who were categorized as "first class" or "global" or "platinum" or "presidential" or "premier" or "executive premier" or "gold and silver club members" or part of the "100,000-mile club" all got to board before everyone else. Some of these customers even got to walk across a six-foot-long red carpet—very impressive. After all these people had boarded, the red carpet was rolled up and put aside and all of us economy class peons were finally allowed to board.

The good news of the Gospel is that Jesus died once for the sins of all of us, regardless of whether we are first class, premier, executive premier, economy class peons or whatever. Jesus died once for all, for all the sin of all people for all time.

The death of Jesus on the cross not only paid the price for all sins for all time, it also is the ultimate proof that God gives us grace, one-way love, all the time. "While we still were sinners," the Bible tells us, "Christ died for us" (Romans 5:8). God is not fickle in his grace towards us; he is constant.

In a recent episode of the TV comedy hit, *The Office*, Dwight Shrute (played brilliantly by Rainn Wilson) is named Acting Manager of the Scranton branch of Dunder-Mifflin. He wreaks havoc during his brief tenure as Manager. At one point in the episode he orders everyone into the conference room and gives them the following speech:

> You guys are my best friends, and I mean that. Managing you for this past week has been the greatest honor of my life. And if you ruin this I will burn this office to the ground... and I mean that figuratively, not literally, because you guys are so important to me. I love you guys, but don't cross me, but you're the best.

This is a hilarious indicator of the problem that sometimes we view God as Dwight Shrute in this speech: neurotically fickle. We wonder where we stand with God and what we have to do to earn or keep God's favor. Fortunately God is nothing like Dwight Shrute.

God is faithful and forgiving. Jesus Christ has already died once for all for all of our sins. We have been given, freely given, grace through Jesus Christ. Through trust in Jesus Christ and his "once for all" death on the cross for us we have been made righteous in God's eyes. Although many of us can sometimes be as neurotic and fickle as Dwight Shrute, God is never that way. God is faithful and forgiving.

Jesus has already suffered for our sins in our place. All we have to do is put our trust in him. R.C. Sproul, a scholar and pastor in Florida, says this:

> (God) is just because he requires the penalty for sin to fulfill all righteousness, which righteousness was accomplished by Christ himself... The only ground for our justification, now and forever, is the imputation of the righteousness of Christ to all who believe. This righteousness... comes from outside of us... (and) belongs only to the One who is just, but it is precisely that foreign righteousness that God accounts to us when we put our trust in Jesus (*1-2 Peter*, p. 124-125).

This year rock icon Bob Dylan turned 70, and the magazine *Rolling Stone* featured a fascinating piece, "The 70 Greatest Dylan Songs." At the top of the list is the epic classic *Like a Rolling Stone*. In the final verse Dylan sings "when you ain't got nothing, you got nothing to lose." When it comes to righteousness before God we "ain't got nothing," while Jesus Christ, the Son of God who had it all, gave it all away, even his life, for you and me in order to bring us to God. He suffered in our place, "the righteous for the unrighteous."

In Charles Dickens' classic novel, *A Tale of Two Cities*, set during the French Revolution, one of the main characters, Sydney Carton, is an alcoholic lawyer who struggles with self-confidence and feels that, by and large, his life has been wasted. Motivated by his unrequited love for Lucie Manette, a beautiful blond who eventually marries an aristocrat named Charles Darnay, Carton succeeds in switching places with Darnay, who had been doomed to be beheaded for being an aristocrat.

In the closing scene of the 1935 David Selznick film based on the novel, Carton is brought to the guillotine, and walks alone up the steps. Just before he is beheaded in place of Charles Darnay, the camera pans up above the guillotine and over Paris as Darnay says the famous final lines of the book: "It is a far far better thing that I do than I have ever done; it is a far far better rest that I go to than I have ever known"—an amazingly arresting final scene and a poignant picture of what it looks like for someone to suffer in another's place.

Similarly Jesus Christ, motivated by his love for all of us, suffered for our sins, once for all, to bring us to God. He walked alone to the cross, and after being nailed to it, prayed, "Father forgive them; for they do not know what they are doing" (Luke 23:34).

Jesus suffered in our place in order "to bring us to God."

Jesus was brought before the chief priests and elders to be falsely accused; Jesus was brought before Pilate to be sentenced to death; Jesus was brought before the soldiers to be mocked and beaten; and, finally, Jesus was brought to the cross to be crucified. Jesus was *brought* in all these ways on our behalf, so that he could *bring* you and me to God. We do not bring ourselves to God; we have been brought to God by Jesus Christ.

The Apostle Peter did not just write about this; he lived it. After following Jesus for three years, after witnessing Jesus heal the blind and walk on water and raise the dead, after seeing miracle after miracle and hearing teaching after teaching, Peter, in Jesus' darkest hour, denies him.

But Peter is forgiven and restored by Jesus. Jesus had brought Peter forgiveness, peace, grace, love—Jesus had brought Peter to God, and his life would never be the same. Not too long after writing his two New Testament letters Peter was himself brought to his own cross; but that was not the end of the story, for Peter's eternal destiny had already been secured by Jesus.

And it is the same with you and me. Regardless of the suffering in our lives, regardless of the sins we have done against others and the sins that have been done against us, our eternal destines have been secured by Jesus, who has already suffered for us "once for all."

And in the meantime, in the midst of the suffering and challenges of our lives, many of us long for something even more than a twelve-year old baseball fan longs for a foul ball; we long for forgiveness for the ways we have hurt others, we long for healing for the ways others have hurt us, we long for God to somehow use the foul balls in our lives for good.

The good news of the Gospel is that when it comes to God's grace, just like in baseball, there is no clock. The sin you have committed against others cannot run out the clock against God's grace. The sin that others have committed against you cannot run out the clock against God's grace. And all the suffering in the world caused by sin cannot run out the clock against God's grace. When it comes to God's grace, time will not run out on you, ever, because when it comes to God's grace, *there is no clock.*

Jesus in his "once for all" death on the cross has forgiven you and has secured your eternal destiny. Jesus suffered for all of us, regardless of whether we walk across a red carpet at an airport, whether we are as broken and wounded as Will Hunting or as fickle as Dwight Shrute or as life-weary as Sydney Carton.

When it comes to suffering for sin, there are no more outs to be made, no more runs to score: "For Christ suffered for sins once for all, the righteous for the unrighteous, in order to bring you to God."

And at the end of human history, when the risen Jesus returns, we will experience the joy of being *brought, once for all*, to heaven, an eternal home where we will forever enjoy a "far, far better rest than we have ever known."

Amen.

NO TAKE-BACKS
T.S. Eliot and the Irrevocable Hostess Cupcake

...for the gifts and the calling of God are irrevocable (Romans 11:29).

In the Name of the Father, Son, and Holy Spirit.

When I was a kid in elementary school there were certain rules you lived by, a code that, if breached, would make you vulnerable to the wrath of the other kids at school. One of these rules, of course, was *no cutting in line*. Sure, it was permissible to scramble to get as close to the front of the line as possible, but once the line was established, there was to be no cutting. Another rule was no trying to be the teacher's pet. Sure, it was permissible to be civil with your teacher, even friendly in extreme cases, but there were to be no overt acts to earn the teacher's favor, at least in front of the class.

Another rule was *no take-backs*. This meant that once you gave something away, you could not ask for it back. "No take-backs" applied to every case when a classmate gave away a valuable commodity to another classmate, like a pencil or magic marker, a baseball card, a finely crafted paper football, or the rarely gifted Snack Pack or Hostess Cupcake. If you gave one of these valuable commodities away, there was to be no asking for it back. If someone asked for it back the offended party would simply say, "No take-backs," and that was the end of it. If not, doom awaited you on the playground.

Today I am preaching on a verse from the lesson from Romans 11:29 in which Paul writes, "The gifts and the calling of God are irrevocable." The gifts and the calling of God are irrevocable. To be irrevocable means not to be recalled or changed. To be irrevocable means unable to be repealed or annulled or undone. Irrevocable means *no take-backs*.

"The gifts and the calling of God are irrevocable," Paul writes. At this point in his Letter to the Romans Paul is describing God's relationship with Israel. He emphasizes that in spite of Israel's disobedience to God, God never took back the gifts he gave them, as he had written earlier in chapter nine: "to (the Israelites) belong the adoption, the glory, the covenants, the giving of the law, the worship, and the promises; to them belong the patriarchs, and from them, according to the flesh, comes the Messiah" (9:4-5).

Throughout the Old Testament we see again and again that God gave these gifts to Israel and did not take them back. We see again and again that God called Israel his chosen people and never took that back. Many of the prominent leaders of the Old Testament were broken sinners, like Jacob who deceived his own brother and father, Moses who had a short temper, Samson who chased prostitutes, David who committed murder and adultery, Hezekiah who catered to the heathen—it goes on and on. And yet in spite of their disobedience God did not disown them. In spite of their unfaithfulness, God remained faithful.

When it came to the gifts and calling God gave to Israel, there were no take-backs. The late biblical scholar F. F. Bruce puts it this way in *Romans*:

> The promises which God made to the patriarchs when he called them are secured to their descendants, not on the ground of merit, but on the ground of God's fidelity to his word of grace (210).

And in today's passage from Romans Paul not only writes, "the gifts and the calling of God are irrevocable," he continues by emphasizing the mercy of God:

> Just as you (Gentiles) were once disobedient to God but have now received mercy because of (Israel's) disobedience, so they have now been disobedient in order that, by the mercy shown to you, they too may now receive mercy. For God has imprisoned all in disobedience so that he may be merciful to all (11:30-32).

In other words, when it comes to Israel, *God's mercy is the final word.*

And this is not just the case with Israel, but with you and me, too. This is good news, because our life experience is replete with take-backs. When it comes to the gifts people give one another, there are often strings attached. And these take-backs often involve things much more important than baseball cards and cupcakes.

Sometimes a company will take back an offer made to an excited new employee and offer the job to someone else. Sometimes the gifts people give one another are yoked to unspoken expectations and run the risk of being taken back. Take-backs often occur in relationships. In his song, *Lonesome Day*, Bruce Springsteen articulates the heartbreak this creates:

> Once I thought I knew
> Everything I needed to know about you
> Your sweet whisper, your tender touch
> But I didn't really know that much
> Joke's on me
> It's gonna be okay
> If I can just get through this lonesome day

Paul Harding's Pulitzer Prize winning novel, *Tinkers* (2009) describes the internal reminiscences of an old man named George Crosby on his deathbed. Crosby, like many of us, experiences take-backs in his life, and is trying to make sense of it all. Early in the novel Harding writes:

> George Crosby remembered many things as he died, but in an order he could not control. To look at his life, to take the stock he always imagined a man would at his end, was to witness a shifting mass, the tiles of a mosaic spinning, swirling, re-portraying, always in recognizable swaths of colors, familiar elements, molecular units, intimate currents, but also independent now of his will, showing him a different self every time he tried to make an assessment (18).

As it is with George, so our life experience can be confusing and non-linear, and the take-backs in our lives only increase the difficulty of assessing it all. And not only are the things people say often revocable, but the events in our lives are *ir*revocable: we cannot turn back the clock and undo or redo things.

In T. S. Eliot's play, *The Family Reunion*, one of the main characters Agatha is anticipating the painful and awkward return of her nephew Harry who has not seen the family in eight years, and is begrudgingly returning home for his mother's birthday:

> I mean painful because everything is irrevocable,
> Because the past is irremediable,
> Because the future can only be built
> Upon the real past.

In some ways Agatha is exactly right: "Everything is irrevocable." What's done is done.

Last week my wife Steph and I dropped our oldest daughter off at college, and it really hit us that her childhood is over. It went by so quickly. One minute we're reading *Good Night Moon* to her before rocking her to sleep, the next we're walking her to Kindergarten. We turn around and we're coaching her in soccer or basketball and buying her ice cream after she gets her braces on. A minute later we're helping her with homework and then hoping she doesn't ask for help because the classes she's taking are beyond us. The next thing we know we're driving her to her high school graduation and then dropping her off at college. It doesn't really matter if we would want to go back in time and undo or redo anything as parents. Her childhood is over. What's done is done.

So we see that on the one hand our lives are filled with take-backs, promises that apparently are revocable; and on the other hand the past events in our lives are *ir*revocable; what's done is done. This can leave our hearts hard, unwilling to believe that there are no take-backs with God, that the gifts and the calling of God really are irrevocable, that God's mercy is the final word. It just sounds too good to be true.

But it is true.

For God has given all of us the greatest gift of all in Jesus Christ who died on the cross for our sins, as Jesus himself said: "For God so loved the world that he gave his only Son, so that everyone who believes in him may not perish but may have eternal life" (John 3:16).

A couple weeks ago the Discovery Channel celebrated *Shark Week*, an entire week packed with documentaries about sharks. My family loves *Shark Week*. One evening we gathered around to watch yet another documentary and the following disclaimer appeared on the screen: "This program contains actual video of real events and acts of foolishness that may be disturbing to some viewers. Viewer discretion is advised."

Our lives are filled with "acts of foolishness" that are irrevocable. But the good news of the Gospel is that out of love for all of us Jesus Christ gave his life for us on the cross, an act the Greeks of his day considered utter foolishness, but as Paul wrote to the Corinthians: "God's foolishness is wiser than human wisdom" and Jesus' death on the cross is "the power of God and the wisdom of God" (1 Corinthians 1:22-25).

While Jesus' death on the cross is "disturbing to some viewers," it is the final and ultimate expression of the irrevocable, foolish love of God for us.

Jesus' death on the cross is the event of "the real past" upon which the present and future of the spinning mosaics of our lives are built. All the take-backs of your life, all the irrevocable past events of your life, all the acts of foolishness of your life are covered, completely covered, by the irrevocable love of Jesus Christ. What's done is done.

The good news of the Gospel is that indeed "the gifts and the calling of God are irrevocable," that God's mercy is the final word, that when it comes to God's love for us, there are no take-backs.

Amen.

SCRAMBLING TO BE FIRST
Christ's Freedom in the Rat Race

So the last will be first, and the first will be last (Matthew 20:16).

In the Name of the Father, Son, and Holy Spirit.

One of my favorite teachers in elementary school was my third grade teacher, Mrs. Stevens, an "old school" teacher who maintained a strict sense of order in class, but who also genuinely cared about each of us. On the first day of school she asked us to line up for lunch and there was a mad scramble to get to the front of the line. After we had lined up, Mrs. Stevens went to the back of the line, smiled and said, "This is the front of the line," and led the class to lunch. I still remember the surprised grin on the face of kid who suddenly found herself in the *front* of the line, as well as the angry response from someone at the back of the line: "This is *so* annoying!"

The next day when we lined up for lunch we all scrambled to be last in line, so Mrs. Stevens went to the middle of the line and said, "Today this is the front of the line." Eventually we all got the message and the scrambling to be first stopped.

Today's Gospel lesson, the Parable of the Landowner, is unsettling on the surface for many people, and for some people their response to this parable is the same as that of the kid in the back of the line: "This is *so* annoying!"

This parable can indeed be annoying because when it comes to merit, to getting what you've earned thank-you-very-much, it turns everything upside down. The grace the landowner demonstrates in this parable is the opposite of what Jesus' hearers, and we, would expect. One scholar aptly refers to this parable as "The Parable of the Eccentric Employer."

We live in a world in which people scramble to be first all the time: kids in elementary school scrambling to be first in the lunch line, high school students scrambling to be in the top ten percent of their class, college students scrambling to get into a certain fraternity or sorority, employees scrambling for promotions, parents scrambling to get their kids ahead.

Every day as I drive down Route 29 on the way here, I find myself scrambling in traffic—that, of course, is one of the areas in my life where my "Christ-like character" is *most* apparent. I've even heard that people scramble to find parking here on Sundays. In the world we live in the scrambling to be first never stops. It goes on and on and on.

But in the kingdom of heaven it is different. In the kingdom of heaven scrambling to be first doesn't work.

In this parable Jesus talks about a landowner who needs workers for his vineyard and one day goes into town multiple times and hires workers for his vineyard. Some work all day, others half a day, others a quarter of a day and still others for just one hour. At the end of the day the landowner does two things that reveal his grace. First, he pays the last people he hired—those who only worked an hour— before anyone else; second, he pays them a full days' wages. He then proceeds to pay everyone else the exact same amount, including those who had worked all day long.

While apparently those who worked less than a full day respond gratefully by accepting the grace of the landowner and going on their merry way, there is an angry, visceral response by those who are paid last. Jesus says, "They grumbled against the landowner" and complain to his face, "These last worked only one hour, and you have made them equal to us who have borne the burden of the day and the scorching heat." These grumbling workers feel entitled.

Listen to how the landowner responds to one of them, perhaps the unofficial leader of the group:

> Friend, I am doing you no wrong; did you not agree with me for the usual daily wage? Take what belongs to you and go; I choose to give to this last the same as I give to you. Am I not allowed to do what I choose with what belongs to me?

In addressing this worker as "Friend" it appears that the landowner is being kind and patient, but the Greek word used here for friend is only used two other times in the entire New Testament: once in the Parable of the Wedding Banquet when a man without the proper garments was thrown out of a wedding (Matthew 22:12) and the other when Jesus addressed Judas at the moment of his betrayal (Matthew 26:50). In other words, the word "friend" in this parable is used not as a compliment, but a rebuke. In all three occurrences of this word in the New Testament, "friend" refers to someone who is opposed to the grace of God.

The landowner continues by emphasizing that he pays according to his own choice, not the entitlement of the angry laborer: "*I choose* to give to this last the same as I give to you. Am I not allowed to do what *I choose* with what belongs to me?"

But the angry entitled laborers were more concerned about their rank than anything else. Listen again to what their representative said: "These last worked only one hour, and *you have made them equal to us* who have borne the burden of the day and the scorching heat" (Talk about a martyr complex).

The angry laborers felt they outranked those who had only worked for an hour, and were furious with the idea of being viewed as equal by the landowner. They were preoccupied with rank and opposed to grace.

It is the same with us. We too can be preoccupied with rank and opposed to God's grace. But the truth is that in God's eyes we are all sinners in need of grace. No one outranks anyone else. We are all in the same boat.

One spring in the 90s when I was serving as a youth minister in South Carolina, I took some high school students on a canoe trip. We picked up our canoes early in the morning and received "training" in the form of a five-minute video on a fuzzy TV. We loaded our canoes and started down the river. About an hour into the trip the current became noticeably stronger. There had been a lot of rain over the winter and spring and while there were many trees on either side of the river, there was no shore; the high water covered the low country as far as you could see.

The kids in one of our canoes ventured too close to the trees and got pinned against them by the strong current. The groups in our other two canoes paddled toward them to help out and we all ended up pinned against the trees by the current. We spent perhaps an hour trying to unpin the canoes, but with no land onto which to stand or unload, and with no way to overcome the strong current, we realized it was impossible for us. We were in the middle of nowhere in the pre-cell phone era with no way to contact anyone for help. One of the kids asked me, "What do we do now?" I thought, *Good question.*

We ended up abandoning the canoes and, with our life-vests on, held onto one another and floated down the river together. The water was very dark and one of the kids said, "I'm petrified of snakes—there aren't any snakes around here, right?" So I did what any youth minister would do in that situation, I lied. "Right," I grinned, "No snakes."

For a couple hours we floated down the river as a clump of refugees, holding onto one another's life vests, at the mercy of the current, with no land in sight. We were all in the same situation—the smart kids and the clueless kids, the athletic and non- athletic kids, the leaders with lots of wilderness experience and the couch potatoes who preferred air-conditioning—all floating down the river, all equally in need of help.

Finally we came to a place where there was actually a bank, and we got out of the river and hiked until we found a road and eventually flagged down some help. At the end of the day we were all fine, and for years after that the kids on that trip laughed with me about it.

When it comes to being sinners in need of God's grace, we are all in (or all out, in this scenario) the same boat. We are all floating helplessly down the dark currents, with no place to get out. In that situation there is no scrambling to be first, and no one outranks anyone else.

And yet this parable is so counterintuitive, so different from what we are used to. We are often just like the entitled workers in this parable: we want pay scale, rank, races to be first. Even in church people often find this parable to be quite annoying.

But in the kingdom of heaven God's grace supersedes all such scrambling—as the Anglican bishop and scholar Michael Green puts it in *The Message of Matthew*: "All human merit shrivels before (God's) burning, self-giving love. Grace, amazing grace, is the burden of this story... There are no rankings in the kingdom of God" (212).

When I went through the process for ordination over ten years ago, I spent hours on my spiritual autobiography, took a battery of psychological and personality tests, read and prepared for the questions I would be asked by various committees over the course of the process, jumped through hoop after hoop. But there was one question that I was asked during one interview that undermined all my preparation, that undermined any sense of entitlement I had going into the process. And the question was: "What is the greatest failure in your life and how did you experience God's grace in that?"

I was completely caught off guard by the question because, frankly, I still had a very narrow view of God's grace at that point in my life. I had yet to learn that the church is not a club for self-righteous superstars but a fellowship of failures who have experienced, and continue to experience, God's grace.

And I know I'm not alone, for many of us still want to cling to our sense of deservedness. Shaking off our sense of deservedness is like trying to shake off a spider web we've walked into, and we don't really want to shake it off anyway. But again, in the kingdom of heaven, God's grace supersedes it all. In his book, *The Ragamuffin Gospel*, Brennan Manning describes this:

> The gospel of grace... obliterates the two-class citizenship theory operative in many American churches. For grace proclaims the awesome truth that all is gift. All that is good is ours, not by right, but by the sheer bounty of a gracious God... Jesus comes not for the super-spiritual but for the wobbly and the weak-kneed who know they don't have it all together, and who are not too proud to accept the handout of amazing grace (25, 28).

Arguably one of the greatest American short story writers is the late Flannery O'Connor. In a letter she once described the main theme of her stories, grace. "Part of the difficulty," she wrote, "is that you write for an audience who doesn't know what grace is and doesn't recognize it when they see it. All my stories are about the action of grace on a character who is not very willing to support it."

O'Connor was only thirty-nine when she died of lupus. Toward the end of her life as her suffering increased she wrote a short story entitled "Revelation," in which she describes Ruby Turpin, a smug self-righteous Southern woman who experiences grace, but as a "character who is not very willing to support it." Near the end of the story Ruby has the following vision:

> She saw the streak as a vast swinging bridge extending upward from the earth through a field of living fire. Upon it a vast horde of souls were rumbling toward heaven. There were whole companies of white trash, clean for the first time in their lives... and battalions of freaks and lunatics shouting and clapping and leaping like frogs. And bringing up the end of the procession was a tribe of people whom she recognized at once as those who, like herself... had always had a little of everything and the God-given wit to use it

right... They were marching behind the
others with great dignity... yet she could see
by their shocked and altered faces that even
their virtues were being burned away... In
the woods around her the invisible cricket
choruses had struck up, but what she heard
were the voices of the souls climbing upward
into the starry field and shouting hallelujah.

In this vision the smug Ruby Turpin finds herself at the end
of the line, behind the white trash, behind the freaks, behind
the lunatics—not unlike the angry, entitled laborers at the
end of the line behind those who had not borne the heat of
the day. In the kingdom of heaven, scrambling for first
doesn't work.

The "annoying" Parable of the Landowner reveals the good
news of the Gospel, that God is a gracious God, that he has
the power to give his grace however and to whomever he
chooses and that he has chosen to give his grace to you and
me, especially in the areas of our greatest failure.

Out of unstoppable love for us Jesus Christ was swept by the
current of our sin and pinned to the cross where he died for
all of us: those who have borne the heat of the day as well as
those who work for only one hour, the angry and entitled
"friends" who oppose the grace of God as well as "the wobbly
and the weak-kneed who know they don't have it all
together," those who welcome God's grace as well as
"characters who are not very willing to support it."

In the kingdom of heaven the first will be last and the last
will be first. God's grace supersedes all scrambling to be
first, all entitlement, all rank because Jesus Christ is the first
and the last, the Alpha and the Omega, who died on the cross
for all of us, and who even now, in the midst of the
scrambling in our lives, offers his grace to us anew. God is
the "eccentric employer" who offers himself freely to us, the
fellowship of failures. And because of the abundant grace

God has given us we will one day join Ruby Turpin and the "clapping and leaping" throngs "climbing upward into the starry field and shouting hallelujah."

Amen.

THE GENTLENESS
OF JESUS CHRIST
McFly's Solace in a World of Biffs

Let your gentleness be known to everyone
(Philippians 4:5).

In the Name of the Father, Son, and Holy Spirit.

Today I will be preaching from the fourth chapter of Philippians. The church at Philippi was the first church in Europe and was founded by Paul during his second missionary journey (Acts 16:11-40). Paul had a special affection for the church at Philippi and in 62 A.D. while imprisoned in Rome, he wrote them the letter that eventually became a part of the New Testament.

Often sermons on the fourth chapter of Philippians focus on rejoicing ("Rejoice in the Lord always; again I will say, *Rejoice*") or prayer ("Do not worry about anything, but in everything *by prayer and supplication* with thanksgiving let your requests be made known to God") or peace ("The *peace* of God, which surpasses all understanding, will guard your hearts and your minds in Christ Jesus"). This sermon, however, will be on an oft-overlooked verse in this passage, verse five, in which Paul writes, "Let your gentleness be known to everyone."

Paul did not instruct the church at Philippi, "Let your passion be known to everyone" or "Let your intensity be known to everyone" or "Let your beautiful buildings and stellar programs be known to everyone;" but rather, "Let your *gentleness* be known to everyone."

We live in a world short on gentleness. Think about your life for a moment. How often are you treated with gentleness? Or how often you are treated harshly or in a way that is overbearing or manipulative or controlling? I bet the latter is more common for you than the former. The world is full of bullies.

When I was in kindergarten I rode the bus to school, and every morning I had a knot in my stomach as I walked to the bus stop because there was a bully awaiting me there named Eric. He got a real *thrill* out of pushing me around, making fun of my crooked teeth, knocking my lunch out my hands and doing other kind and wonderful things that helped a kindergartner's day get off to a great start. When the bus arrived at school I would sprint past Eric and into the school building and when the bus arrived back to the bus stop after school I would sprint past Eric and run home, every single day.

And you know from your own life that the bullying does not stop in kindergarten. I imagine that even now each of you can recall specific bullies from elementary school or the mean girls or angst-ridden bullies of high school (two film examples: Cady Heron's foe Regina in *Mean Girls,* and George McFly's tormentor, Biff in *Back to the Future*). As adults, how many of you have worked for a bully, a belittler, a control freak?

Or perhaps you can think of marriages in which husbands bully wives with their narcissism, or in which wives bully their husbands with their passive-aggression. Perhaps you can think of parents who bully their children in various ways.

There's even church bullying. There are bully clergy who preach bully sermons from bully pulpits, who treat people in the church as cogs in their self-centered ministry machine. On the flip-side there are clergy who are bullied by influential lay leaders, who consistently undermine them and want to see them fail. Some years ago I had a friend who was a priest—faithful, kind, gifted—who was bullied by the lay leadership in his church for ten years straight. He burned out and left the ministry.

All of us know what it's like to walk reluctantly with knots in our stomachs to the various bus stops in our lives or how tiring it can be to try and outrun the bullies. All this bullying can leave us in a place where we long for some gentleness.

In the late 80s five rock 'n' roll icons—Dylan, Petty, Lynne, Orbison, and Harrison—formed a band they called the Travelling Wilburys. Their biggest hit, "Handle with Care", expresses this longing for gentleness. Here are some of the lyrics:

> Been beat up and battered 'round
> Been sent up, and I've been shot down
> You're the best thing that I've ever found
> Handle me with care

> I've been fobbed off, and I've been fooled
> I've been robbed and ridiculed
> In daycare centers and night schools
> Handle me with care

Been stuck in airports, terrorized
Sent to meetings, hypnotized
Overexposed, commercialized
Handle me with care

When I was in middle school I attended a very strict Christian school. Allow me to juxtapose two teachers from that school. Teacher number one: The Bible Teacher was a big intimidating former football coach. One day during class I was sitting in my usual place, the very back row, cutting up with one of my friends. Suddenly the teacher stopped talking and a scared silence filled the room, and I noticed he was glaring at me. Without taking his eyes off me, he slowly walked to where I was sitting, grabbed my shirt, and stood me up on my tip toes. Without letting go of my shirt he led me through the rows to an empty chair in the middle of the front row and sat me down. He told me that was my new permanent seat. As you can imagine, I learned all sorts of "helpful" theology in that class.

Teacher number two: The Latin Teacher was a soft-spoken man. Latin was one of my favorite classes, not so much because I enjoyed declining nouns and conjugating verbs, but because there was a stunning girl named Lisa in the class, and I had the privilege of sitting in the desk right behind hers. During one class, although the teacher was giving an inspired lecture on the pluperfect tense, I began writing a long note to Lisa. Gushing poetically about her beauty and completely absorbed by my emerging masterpiece, suddenly I found Latin Teacher's hand on my desk. I watched in helpless horror as he took the note away. His policy was if he caught you passing a note in class he would, yes, read it aloud to the class, and our class had heard him read many a juicy note. There was precedent, and now it was my turn, and I didn't turn red, I turned purple. The teacher silently read the note, all of it, the class eagerly waiting to hear it read. After a moment, he paused and smiled, slowly folding it and putting it in his pocket, and gently said, "Nicely done, but if you could focus on Latin for a few minutes I'd really appreciate it." That was it. I would have conjugated a thousand verbs for that man.

Two teachers, the one intimidated me in the name of Jesus; the other treated me with the gentleness of Jesus. I imagine you could share similar stories.

Here's the good news: Jesus is not a bully. Jesus is gentle. Jesus handles us with care.

In his earthly ministry, Jesus was moved with compassion for people who were bullied, people who "were harassed and helpless, like sheep without a shepherd" (Matthew 9:36). That's why people were drawn to him, especially those who had been bullied. Lepers whom most people would not even acknowledge, Jesus would gently touch. Little children, whom the disciples simply wanted to be rid of, were gently welcomed by Jesus into his arms. To a woman caught in adultery whom the Pharisees wanted to stone to death, Jesus gently said, "Neither do I condemn you... go and sin no more."

Jesus was gentle and handled people with care; he would "not break a bruised reed or quench a smoldering wick" (Matthew 12:20); he was sent "to proclaim release to the captives" and "to let the oppressed go free" (Luke 4:18). Instead of bullying the weak and oppressed, Jesus stood up for them and warned the bullying Pharisees against burdening them with their legalism.

Jesus was gentle and handled people with care. "Come to me, all you that are weary and are carrying heavy burdens," he said, "and I will give you rest. Take my yoke upon you, and learn from me; for I am *gentle*... and you will find rest for your souls" (Matthew 11:28-29).

Jesus did not say, "Learn from me, for I am intense" or "Learn from me, for I am overbearing" or "Learn from me, for I am intimidating" or "Learn from me, for I am manipulative."

"Learn from me for I am *gentle*," he said, "and you will find rest for your souls."

In response to the gentleness with which Jesus treats us, we are called to be gentle with others: "Let your gentleness be known to everyone," Paul writes.

This is the work of the Holy Spirit. In the same way the Holy Spirit enables us to love others in response to God loving us (John 15:12) and to welcome others in response to God welcoming us (Romans 15:7) and to forgive others in response to God forgiving us (Ephesians 4:32), the Holy Spirit bears the fruit of gentleness in our lives and helps us to be gentle with others in response to God's being gentle with us. In his Letter to the Galatians Paul describes the fruit of the Spirit as not only love, joy and peace, but also *gentleness* (5:23).

"Let your gentleness be known to everyone."

When I was in seminary a homiletics professor once remarked that the role of a good preacher is to "afflict the comfortable and comfort the afflicted." I dutifully wrote it down in my notebook—very catchy, and on the surface it sounded exactly right. There was a time when I tried to do just that when I preached: "afflict the comfortable and comfort the afflicted."

But I have learned, both in my life and in ministry that, while it is catchy, it is also completely wrong. The reason it is wrong is quite simple: no one is truly comfortable, at least no one I have ever met. Everyone I have ever gotten to know below the surface is anything *but* comfortable. Everyone I have ever gotten to know below the surface feels afflicted in one way or another, either from bullies without or the bully within, who of course is often the cruelest bully of all.

That's why Jesus was gentle and handled people with care; that's why Jesus was moved to compassion when he saw the crowds who were harassed and helpless like sheep without a shepherd; that's why Jesus said, "Learn from me, for I am *gentle*."

The good news of the Gospel is that Jesus was bullied on your behalf, that Jesus was afflicted on your behalf.

On Palm Sunday Jesus did not enter Jerusalem as an imposing bully on an even more imposing steed, but rather "*gentle* and riding on a donkey" (Matthew 21:25, citing Zechariah 9:9), and as he rode into Jerusalem that day he was fully aware that there were many bullies waiting at the bus stop. We know from his anguish in the Garden of Gethsemane that his stomach was in knots.

Jesus was bullied on your behalf. He was bullied by the religious leaders who falsely accused him of blasphemy. He was bullied by the crowd who chanted, "Crucify him! Crucify him!" He was bullied by the Roman soldiers who pounded a crown of thorns into his head and nailed him to a cross.

And yet even then Jesus was still gentle. "Father, forgive them," he said, "They do not know what they are doing."

Even as he hung helplessly on the cross Jesus was still bullied as those who passed by mocked him, "If you are the Son of God, come down from the cross!" Even one of the criminals between whom he was crucified bullied him, "Are you not the Messiah? Save yourself and us!"

The bullying never stopped for Jesus, until his last breath, when he gently said, "Father, into your hands I commend my spirit," and died. Gentle Jesus was bullied on your behalf, dying for every instance in which you have been bullied or bullied others or bullied yourself. He has gently folded it all up and put it into his pocket.

Jesus was even gentle after his resurrection, after which he went to the room where the disciples were hiding, the same disciples who ran away in his darkest hour, and gently said, "Peace be with you." He continued to handle the disciples with care.

And it is the same with us. Jesus is gentle and handles us with care. He is the Good Shepherd whom the Bible tells us *gently* leads us (Isaiah 40:11). This is the case right this moment, and it will always be the case.

When I was a senior in high school my favorite class was English Literature, and I remember being particularly moved by a famous poem, "Do Not Go Gentle into That Good Night," by the Welsh poet Dylan Thomas:

> Do not go gentle into that good night,
> Old age should burn and rave at close of day;
> Rage, rage against the dying of the light.
>
> Though wise men at their end know dark is right,
> Because their words had forked no lightning they
> Do not go gentle into that good night.
>
> Good men, the last wave by, crying how bright
> Their frail deeds might have danced in a green bay,
> Rage, rage against the dying of the light.
>
> Wild men who caught and sang the sun in flight,
> And learn, too late, they grieved it on its way,
> Do not go gentle into that good night.
>
> Grave men, near death, who see with blinding sight
> Blind eyes could blaze like meteors and be gay,
> Rage, rage against the dying of the light.
>
> And you, my father, there on the sad height,
> Curse, bless, me now with your fierce tears, I pray.

Do not go gentle into that good night.
Rage, rage against the dying of the light.

The reality is that all of us—the wise, the good, the wild, the grave, our fathers, all of us—on a day and hour known only to God will go into that good night, gently or otherwise. And in this life we are often not treated with gentleness. Bullying abounds. That's the bad news.

But the good news is that although bullying abounds, Jesus' gentleness abounds all the more, and he gives us grace in those places where we are bullied. The good news is that we don't have to rage against the dying of the light because Jesus, the Light of the World, has already endured the full fury of that rage in our place.

The good news is that, when we arrive at our final bus stop, we will not be greeted by bullies, but by the risen Jesus, who will gently wipe every tear from our eyes and welcome us home, where we will experience eternal rest for our souls.

Amen.

GOD'S DESTINY FOR YOU
What It Means When It Doesn't Go the Way You Thought It Should

For God has destined us not for wrath but for obtaining salvation through our Lord Jesus Christ, who died for us, so that whether we are awake or asleep we may live with him (1 Thessalonians 5:9-10).

In the Name of the Father, Son, and Holy Spirit.

Today I'm preaching from the fifth chapter of Paul's first Letter to the Thessalonians, which many scholars believe was Paul's earliest letter, written around 50 AD. The church at Thessalonica was founded by Paul during his second missionary journey (Acts 17:1-9), and the believers there, like many of us, struggled with their understanding of various aspects of the Christian faith, particularly the Resurrection and the Second Coming. In response to these struggles Paul wrote to clarify these issues and encourage them in their faith.

One of the topics of the fifth chapter of 1 Thessalonians is *destiny*. Destiny has to do with how the events of our lives fit together and what the future holds for us.

Some childhood prodigies seem destined for greatness. Most high school yearbooks include pictures of those voted "most likely to succeed." Some people seem to have fortunate destinies, others tragic ones.

Destiny is one of the main themes of the classic 1994 Oscar-winning film, *Forrest Gump*. Early in the film the young Forrest asks his mom, "What's my destiny, Mama?" to which she responds, "You're gonna have to figure that out for yourself."

Later in the film another character, Lieutenant Dan, who had believed his destiny was to die in the glory of battle but had been rescued by Forrest, is recuperating in a veteran's hospital, having had both legs amputated. One night he angrily yells at Forrest about how his destiny had not unfolded according to his plan:

> Now, you listen to me. We all have a destiny. Nothing just happens; it's all part of a plan. I should have died out there with my men! But now, I'm nothing but a cripple! A legless freak. Look! Look! Look at me! Do you see that?... You cheated me. I had a destiny. I was supposed to die in the field! With honor! That was my destiny! And you cheated me out of it! You understand what I'm saying, Gump? This wasn't supposed to happen. Not to me. I had a destiny.

Near the conclusion of the film Forrest is standing at the grave of his wife, and says, "Jenny, I don't know if Momma was right or if it's Lieutenant Dan. I don't know if we each have a destiny, or if we're all just floating around accidental-like on a breeze, but I think maybe it's both."

This film hit a nerve for many people, because at different times in our lives we may feel like our destinies are up to us, or that we are indeed "just floating around accidental-like on a breeze." At other times we experience seasons in our lives in which, like Lieutenant Dan, we think, "This wasn't supposed to happen. Not to me. I had a destiny."

Some view one's destiny as being completely up to the individual. William Jennings Bryan—the famous politician of the early 20th century, was of this ilk, declaring with great confidence, "Destiny is not a matter of chance, it is a matter of choice; it is not a thing to be waited for: it is a thing to be achieved." Many people agree with this philosophy. It's great fodder for motivational speeches. Of course, things still didn't go according Bryan's plan; he ran for the presidency three times and lost each time.

Sigmund Freud had a more concise and focused view on the topic of destiny, writing simply: "Anatomy is destiny." *Thank you, Siggy.*

In 1 Thessalonians 5:9-10 Paul writes about destiny, and differs significantly with Forrest Gump, William Jennings Bryan and even Sigmund Freud as he wrote the following, "God has destined us not for wrath but for obtaining salvation through our Lord Jesus Christ, who died for us, so that whether we are awake or asleep we may live with Him."

God has destined you not for wrath, but for obtaining salvation through our Lord Jesus Christ.

This ties into what is known as the Doctrine of Predestination, a doctrine that makes many people in the church squirm—not exactly a topic for coffee hour. And yet predestination is biblical. In the back of *The Book of Common Prayer* under the section, "Historical Documents of the Church" (not to be confused with a different section, the always funny "Hysterical Documents of the Church") you can find the Thirty-nine Articles, the classic doctrinal statement of the English Reformation. Article 17 states the following about predestination:

> Predestination to Life is the everlasting purpose of God, whereby (before the foundations of the world were laid) he hath constantly decreed by his counsel secret... to bring (people) by Christ to everlasting salvation, as vessels made to honour... the godly consideration of Predestination, and our Election in Christ, is full of sweet, pleasant, and unspeakable comfort to godly persons, and such as feel in themselves the working of the Spirit of Christ *(BCP, 871)*.

Notice how Article 17 begins, "Predestination *to Life* is the everlasting purpose of God." That is exactly what we see in 1 Thessalonians 5: "God has destined us not for wrath but for obtaining salvation through our Lord Jesus Christ." And this truth is not intended to foster paranoia or cynicism, but rather, as Article 17 puts it, "sweet, pleasant, and unspeakable comfort."

Often people squirm when it comes to predestination because they focus on the idea of people being predestined to hell. Similarly, back in the late 90s, a flea market operator in Kingsville, Texas named Leonoso Canales led a campaign to change the greeting "hello" into "heaveno" (I'm not making this up): "I see 'hell' in the word 'hello,'" he wrote, "It's disguised by the 'o,' but once you see it, it will slap you in the face."

Similarly people often see "hell" when it comes to the Doctrine of Predestination, and sometimes confuse the Doctrine of Predestination with what is known as *Double-Predestination*, that God has predestined some to heaven and others to hell. In other words, Double-Predestination is the idea that Christ only died on the cross for the sins of the elect and that God has created some people and predestined them to hell to his glory.

This is not found in the Bible. The Bible is clear that Christ died on the cross for *all* of us, that God wants no one to perish but *all* to come to repentance, and that Christ suffered once for *all*, the righteous for the unrighteous, to bring us to God. In his book on the Thirty-nine Articles, Anglican bishop and scholar John Rodgers describes this:

> There is no teaching of predestination to hell in Article 17 or in Scripture. Hell is a destiny mankind has chosen for itself in the Fall. And we, as children of Adam, reiterate the Fall by our own sin. Anglicans have generally held that a doctrine of predestination unto Hell, or double predestination, is a false teaching. To teach that God created persons in order to condemn them, so as to have occasion to reveal his justice, is foreign to Scripture, dishonors God, and is a false doctrine. Predestination to life... is good news for sinners (*Essential Truths for Christians*, 337).

Again, the good news is that God has predestined us to life, that again, as Paul wrote in today's passage: "God has destined us not for wrath but for obtaining salvation through our Lord Jesus Christ."

And yet, unfortunately, there are some people who may refuse God's gift of life through Jesus Christ. There are some who, like the older brother in Jesus' parable of the Prodigal Son, would rather skip the party of grace and stand alone in the courtyard, arms crossed in self-righteousness. But the Bible is clear that God has predestined us to life, not death.

I must confess that years ago I put a lot more stock in free will than predestination, but after years of experience in life and ministry—both good and bad—I've come to maintain a very low view of free will and an increasingly high view of God's sovereignty. I think the gifted preacher T. D. Jakes got it right when he said, "If you live long enough, life will shut your mouth."

One of my favorite country music albums is Martina McBride's 2006 album, *Waking Up Laughing*. The finals song is called "Love Land," a beautiful ballad about how God worked out the destiny of a young lady with a checkered past. The song concludes, "Only God could have planned the steps I've taken that led me to where I am, Love Land." Sometimes you can look back on parts of your life and think, "Only God could have worked that out, thank You, God." That's true for me anyway.

Paul then writes that we receive salvation and life "through Jesus Christ, who died for us." The phrase "for us" means "in our behalf" or "in our place." When Jesus died on the cross for us, he endured the wrath due us in our place, on our behalf. When Jesus died for us, it was a "life for life" transaction, his life for ours.

The end of the 2004 film *Man on Fire* brilliantly portrays what a "life for life" transaction looks like. In this film, which is based on a true story, Denzel Washington plays John Creasy, a former CIA operative who is hired to protect a nine-year old girl named Pita, played by Dakota Fanning, who is from a wealthy Mexican family. Under his watch Pita is kidnapped and at the end of the film John accepts the terms for her release, literally exchanging his life for hers. John walks across a bridge and hands himself over to Pita's captors, who simultaneously set Pita free to walk the opposite direction across the bridge and be reunited with her mom. It's an indelibly rich image of life-for-life. And it really happened.

Jesus died for us, life-for-life. It really happened. And this life with God to which we are predestined is to be experienced both now and in heaven, or as Paul puts it in today's passage, "so that whether we are awake or asleep we may live with him."

The fact that God has destined us to life, not wrath, gives us hope, and in 1 Thessalonians 5 Paul compares the hope of salvation, the hope that God indeed has destined us to life not wrath, to a helmet: "Put on... for a helmet the hope of salvation," he writes. Similarly in his description of the "armor of God' in his Letter to the Ephesians, Paul writes, "Take the helmet of salvation" (6:17).

One November years ago when I was serving as a youth minister we did a high school fall retreat in the mountains, and the camp where we stayed had a zip-line that went out over a lake. The way it worked was you put on a life-vest and helmet and you held on to the zip-line and ran down a ramp as fast as you could, and then hummed along over the lake at a fast speed. Eventually you were supposed to let go of the zip-line and drop into the lake and then swim to shore. One of the boys on the trip, a nice kid but not exactly the sharpest tack in the box, took his turn on the zip-line, and completely forgot he was supposed to let go and drop into the lake. I vividly remember watching in horror as he kept humming along the zip-line all the way to end, crashing into the tree around which the zip-line was tied. "That's a rough ride!" he exclaimed as he groggily wobbled to his feet. When everyone realized he was okay we all laughed. Helmets can come in handy.

We need the helmet of the hope of salvation because we tend to forget to let go of the zip-line, because we want to cling to the illusion that we are in ultimate control of our destinies, and often when we do that—we crash.

The good news of the Gospel is that God gives us the helmet of salvation, that God has destined us to life, not wrath, because Jesus Christ died *for us* to make that possible, life-for-life.

So what about your destiny? Perhaps you're young and feel destined to great things and eager to get out there and make it happen, or perhaps you feel like Lieutenant Dan, like you have endured some "This wasn't supposed to happen" experiences in your life. Or perhaps you've misplaced your helmet.

The good news of the Gospel is that "God has destined us not for wrath but for obtaining salvation through our Lord Jesus Christ, who died for us, so that whether we are awake or asleep we may live with him."

The good news is that because Jesus died for you, one day you'll find yourself in heaven, in Love Land. In the meantime, may the Holy Spirit brand this truth in your heart and give you "sweet, pleasant, and unspeakable comfort."

Amen.

GOD OUR COMFORTER
Love in the Age of Credit Card Debt

*Comfort, O comfort my people, says your God.
Speak tenderly to Jerusalem, and cry to her
that she has served her term, that her penalty is
paid (Isaiah 40:1-2).*

In the Name of the Father, Son, and Holy Spirit.

One day I got home from school and my mom and I were
talking. She read the Bible a lot and told me that she had
been reading the Gospel According to Matthew that day and
came across a verse that she felt God wanted her to share
with me. Then she handed me a Bible, the King James
Version (which is, of course, the version Jesus used), and I
read the following verse: "Lord, have mercy on my son, for
he is a lunatic" (Matthew 17:15).

There are 929 chapters in the Old Testament, and today I have the privilege of preaching from my favorite, Isaiah 40. In my opinion Isaiah 40 is one of the most comforting and encouraging chapters of the Bible.

One of the most prolific of the Old Testament prophets was Isaiah, whose ministry was in the 8th century B.C. and lasted about 50 years. His prophecies about the coming Suffering Servant, referring to Jesus Christ, are among the high points in all of Scripture. Today I am preaching from Isaiah 40:1-2—"'Comfort, O comfort my people,' says your God. 'Speak tenderly to Jerusalem... that her penalty is paid.'"

This time of year one of the greatest pieces of classical music ever composed, Handel's *Messiah*, is often performed. George Frideric Handel composed the *Messiah* over the course of only 24 days in the summer of 1741. The lyrics, a combination of scripture texts from the King James Version of the Bible and *The Book of Common Prayer*, were compiled by Charles Jennens. The first words sung in the *Messiah* are directly from Isaiah 40: "Comfort ye, comfort ye my people, saith your God."

To comfort means "to console or reassure." The Hebrew verb *nachamu* translated "comfort" here literally means, "to cause to breathe again." In other words, God is speaking through Isaiah, "You can breathe easy again."

These comforting words from Isaiah 40 applied not only to the people of Israel and Judah back then, but also apply to all of us right now. Sometimes we look to other people to give us that comfort, perhaps a spouse or boyfriend or girlfriend or parent or child. And yet that comfort often falls short, because on one level or another, the other hurts and needs comfort, too. When seeking comfort from others, people can often receive the opposite, *dis*comfort.

Early on in Shakespeare's classic tragedy, *Macbeth*, one of the characters, a Sergeant, looks out at the sea and says comfort often becomes discomfort:

> As whence the sun 'gins his reflection
> Shipwrecking storms and direful thunders break,
> So from that spring whence comfort seem'd to come
> Discomfort swells (Act I, Scene 2).

A powerful example of this in Scripture involves Job. You may remember that Job loses his children, loses his wealth, and loses his health. In the face of all his tremendous loss does Job receive comfort from his wife? Not exactly. When Job turns to his wife for comfort, her response is rather curt: "Curse God, and die."

Job has three friends—Eliphaz, Bildad, and Zophar (all popular kids names nowadays), who hear about Job's sufferings and visit him. Scripture tells us that when they see Job, "They raised their voices and wept aloud (and) sat with him on the ground for seven days and seven nights, and no one spoke a word to him, for they saw that his suffering was very great" (Job 2:12-13).

I imagine that the silent presence of Job's friends for that week brings him some comfort. But then his friends make the mistake of opening their mouths. The ensuing chapters in Job recount their trying to explain to Job that his suffering is brought about by his sin, that in losing his children, wealth, and health, he is getting what he deserves. As you can imagine, Job does not find this very comforting, and eventually tells them bluntly, "Miserable comforters are you all" (16:2). When Job looks to his wife and friends for comfort, "*dis*comfort swells."

Job of course eventually receives comfort, but this comfort does not come from Eliphaz, Bildad, or Zophar. It does not even come from his wife. It comes from God, who eventually restores Job completely.

The reality is that when people suffer and need comfort but receive none, they often begin to feel a deep sense of isolation and abandonment, and then resort to other things for comfort. As a result, all kinds of addictions develop. I don't need to list these addictions; I am sure you can fill in the blank.

For those of you waiting for my rock 'n' roll reference in this sermon, here it is: *The Wall* by Pink Floyd (1979), one of the most popular albums of the 70s, is all about seeking comfort in the midst of pain. At one point on the album David Gilmour sings about addiction: "I have become comfortably numb," and then proceeds to play a jaw-dropping guitar solo of epic proportions.

The problem with becoming "comfortably numb" is that eventually the numbness wears off, the hurt sets in again, and the thing putting off the pain instead only exacerbates the pain later.

And it's not just "addicts," per se, who need comfort— although in my opinion most people are addicted to something even if on the surface it's not evident—everyone needs comfort from time to time.

Little kids need comfort when they're bullied at school— middle and high school students when "friends" post mean things on Facebook, college students when the daunting prospect of final exams and papers surfaces after hundreds of hours of playing *Call of Duty*. Middle-aged people need comfort when they feel stuck on autopilot, simply going through the motions in an attempt to keep up with the demands of life. The elderly need comfort when the reality of their mortality begins to descend on them.

The need for comfort never goes away.

And it goes both directions. Some people want to give comfort to others but for whatever reason are unable to do so. About a month ago in *The New York Times Book Review* I read about a conversation between two literary giants of the 19th century: Fyodor Dostoyevsky and Charles Dickens. The following is from a letter of Dostoyevsky in which he described this conversation:

> He (Charles Dickens) told me that all the good, simple people in his novels... are what he wanted to have been, and his villains were what he was (or rather, what he found in himself), his cruelty, his acts of causeless enmity towards those who were helpless and looked to him for comfort, his shrinking from those whom he ought to love... There were two people in him, he told me: one who feels as he ought to feel and one who feels the opposite.

What a piercing insight into the conflicted human heart. How often have you felt like there were two people in you? How often have people looked to you for comfort and instead you've given them "acts of causeless enmity?"

If you can relate to this, you are certainly not alone. Even the Apostle Paul was conflicted, as he reveals in his Letter to the Romans: "I do not understand my own actions. For I do not do what I want, but I do the very thing I hate" (7:15).

So there's the problem. Most people are in some kind of pain and therefore need comfort, but often they can find no one who isn't *also* seeking comfort in pain.

But this is where the Gospel comes in. Why did God say, "Comfort, O comfort my people?" It is because "(our) penalty is paid," or as it says in the King James Version, "(our) iniquity is pardoned." In other words, the debt for our sins has been paid in full. The Suffering Servant about whom Isaiah prophesied was none other than Jesus Christ, who paid the penalty for all of our sins, who pardoned all our iniquity.

Each year, beginning on Black Friday, people tend to spend a lot of money Christmas shopping, but then the January credit card statements arrive in the mail, and some people nearly fall over when they see how much they owe. On credit card statements, you are shown both the "amount you owe" and the "minimum payment due." The good news of the Gospel is that because of the death of Jesus Christ on the cross the "amount you owe" for your sins is $0.00, and your "minimum payment due" is $0.00. Your sin debt has been paid entirely.

This past summer the great Anglican scholar John Stott died. Interestingly enough, during his final hours do you know what he was listening to? It wasn't Pink Floyd. It was Handel's *Messiah*, "Comfort ye, comfort ye my people... for her iniquity is pardoned."

In his profound book, *The Cross of Christ* Stott wrote about how, in his death on the cross, Jesus paid our sin debt in full:

> God's love must be wonderful beyond comprehension. God could quite justly have abandoned us to our fate. He could have left us alone to reap the fruit of our wrongdoing and to perish in our sins. It is what we deserved. But he did not. Because he loved us, he came after us in Christ. He pursued us even to the desolate anguish of the cross, where he bore our sin, guilt, judgment, and death... It is more than love. Its proper name is 'grace,' which is love to the undeserving. (God) himself in his Son has borne the penalty for (our) law-breaking (83, 190).

And when Jesus suffered and died, he received no comfort at all. When he said he was thirsty, he was offered vinegar on a stick, literally surrounded by miserable comforters. And yet when he died he paid our sin debt entirely so that we could be comforted. In fact, Jesus sent the Holy Spirit to be our Holy *Comforter* (not Holy Lecturer or Holy Motivator), in our places of need. We need to hear this comfort again and again.

That's why immediately following the confession and absolution in the Holy Eucharist, Rite One service in *The Book of Common Prayer* the priest says the "comfortable words," scriptures that remind us that Jesus has indeed paid the debt for our sin. In fact, in the First English Book of Common Prayer, compiled and written by Thomas Cranmer in 1549, the priest was to say the following:

> Hear what *comfortable* words our savior Christ sayeth, to all that truly turn to him. Come unto me all those who travail and are heavy laden, and I shall refresh you. God so loved the world that he gave his only begotten Son, to the end that all that believe in him, should not perish, but have life everlasting.

> Here what St. Paul sayeth. This is a true saying, and worthy of all men to be received, that Jesus Christ came into this world to save sinners.

> Hear also what St. John sayeth. If any man sin, we have an advocate with the father, Jesus Christ the righteous, and he is the propitiation for our sins.

Every week the priest was to comfort the congregation by reading all four of those verses to remind them that they were forgiven, that their sin debt had been paid in full. The reality is that our need to be reminded of this has not changed since 1549.

One more illustration... One of the most comforting songs I have ever heard is Simon and Garfunkel's "Bridge over Troubled Water" from 1970, a song I don't remember ever *not* knowing. In case you were curious it comes in at number

47 on *Rolling Stone's* "500 Greatest Songs of All Time." It is
pure gospel as they sing:

> When you're weary, feeling small
> When tears are in your eyes, I will dry them all
> I'm on your side when times get rough and friends
> just can't be found
> Like a bridge over troubled water
> I will lay me down

> When you're down and out, when you're on the street
> When evening falls so hard, I will *comfort* you
> I'll take your part when darkness comes and pain is
> all around
> Like a bridge over troubled water
> I will lay me down

Paul Simon wrote this final verse for his then wife, Peggy,
who was discouraged because she had recently noticed her
first gray hairs:

> Sail on silver girl, sail on by
> Your time has come to shine, all your dreams are on
> their way
> See how they shine
> When you need a friend, I'm sailing right behind
> Like a bridge over troubled water
> I will ease your mind

The good news of the gospel is that God cares for us when
we're weary and feeling small, that God will comfort us, that
God took our part, that God is sailing right behind,
especially when the waters of *dis*comfort swell.

The good news of the Gospel is that Jesus died for all us, that
the amount we owe on our sin debt is $0.00.

Jesus died for the abandoned and the isolated and the
addicted. Jesus died for lunatics and silver girls, for classical

composers and brilliant playwrights. Jesus died for conflicted novelists and rock 'n' roll icons, for those who need comfort and those who are miserable comforters.

And Jesus also died for *you*, so today you can be reassured— that you have been forgiven, that God loves you all the time, no matter what.

Today you can breathe easy again.

Amen.

MOVED WITH PITY
The Don Johnson We Want To Be and the Valentine Who Did All the Choosing

A leper came to him begging him, and kneeling he said to him, "If you choose, you can make me clean." Moved with pity, Jesus stretched out his hand and touched him, and said to him, "I do choose. Be made clean!" Immediately the leprosy left him, and he was made clean (Mark 1:40-42).

In the Name of the Father, Son, and Holy Spirit.

It's 1986. You're a seventeen-year-old junior in high school and Valentine's Day is on a Friday that year. There's a beautiful sophomore who's caught your eye. Her older sister is a model and she's better looking than her older sister. You go to the store to get her candy—*Russell Stover's or Brach's, Russell Stover's or Brach's?* You go with Russell Stover's, because with the box of Russell Stover's chocolate comes a stuffed bear—*perfect.*

You arrive at school with your game plan: between second and third period you'll see her in the hallway by her locker, give her the bear, the candy, and ask her on a date for that night. You have your speech rehearsed and ready to go. You're crazy about this girl, but you'll be casual, *suave.* As your second period history class is winding down your palms begin to sweat, your heart begins to race.

The bell rings, you enter the hallway and begin walking toward her locker, but she's chatting with a couple friends, and you panic because you had expected a private moment. You stand frozen in the hallway and, before you know it, the bell rings and you tuck the bear and candy back under your Levi's denim jacket and rush off to Trigonometry, thinking to yourself, "No problem, I'll ask her after school."

The final bell rings and you again walk down the hallway toward her locker—palms sweaty and heart racing, yet again—only to see her blushing as she receives some flowers from another guy and smiles at him, "See you tonight," she tells him. As the guy waltzes past you, he gives you a smirk. He's going on a date with her that night; you're not. It's too late. You missed your chance.

You drive home with the bear and candy in the passenger seat, the bear silently staring at you. When you get home you give the bear and candy to your little sister—she thinks you're so nice to do that and you smile and say nothing. Later that night you sit alone in your room feeling so alone as you watch *Miami Vice*, wishing more than anything that you could be as confident and cool as Don Johnson...

Valentine's Day is a mixed bag, isn't it? Going all the way back to elementary school when you had to give Valentines to everyone in your class... which one do you give your best friend? Which one do you give to person you have a crush on? Which one do you give the weird kid in class? (That's the most important because you certainly don't want to send the wrong message to the weird kid…)

All the way into adulthood Valentine's Day can be thrilling for some, riddled with anxiety for others—the flowers and candy usually have strings attached. For still others, Valentine's Day is one of the loneliest days of the year.

In today's lesson from the first chapter of Mark's account of the gospel Jesus encounters someone who was lonely *every* day of the year, a leper. To be a leper in Jesus' day meant you were often alone. If you were a leper, listen to what the Old Testament mandated about you:

> The person who has the leprous disease shall wear torn clothes and let the hair of his head be disheveled; and he shall cover his upper lip and cry out, 'Unclean, unclean.' He shall remain unclean as long as he has the disease… He shall live alone; his dwelling shall be outside the camp (Leviticus 13:45-46).

Imagine not being allowed to touch or be touched by another human being—no hugs, no kisses, no handshakes, no pats on the back, no comforting caresses, no high-fives. Imagine people avoiding you every day, avoiding eye contact as they hurriedly pass you by, parents turning their little kids away from seeing you. Imagine being allowed to attend worship at a synagogue only if you stood behind a screen that isolated you from everyone else, so that no one would even have to look at you.

This is the kind of person who approaches Jesus for help, literally begging on his knees, utterly broken, utterly desperate.

"If you *choose*," the leper says to Jesus, "You can make me clean."

In the Old Testament there are many passages about choosing to serve the Lord, the most well-known being Joshua's charge to Israel: "Choose this day whom you will serve... but as for me and my household, we will serve the Lord" (Joshua 24:15).

That's the Law. Just *choose* to serve God. Just make that choice. But interestingly enough, there is nothing in the New Testament about choosing to serve the Lord or choosing to do much of anything else. Instead, the New Testament emphasizes that God *has chosen* you.

This is grace.

At the Last Supper Jesus, only hours before his death, tells his disciples, "You did *not* choose me but I *chose* you" (John 15:16). The Apostle Paul put it this way: "(God) *chose* us in Christ before the foundation of the world" (Ephesians 1:4). The Apostle Peter put it this way: "You are a *chosen* race" (I Peter 2:9).

Now that we are well into February many people have punted on their New Year's resolutions, things they chose to do or not do this year. Resolutions tend to have a relatively brief shelf life, don't they? Listen to what Oscar Wilde, the brilliant nineteenth century English writer, observes about resolutions in his classic novel, *The Picture of Dorian Gray*:

> Good resolutions are useless attempts to interfere with scientific laws. Their origin is pure vanity. Their result is absolutely nil... They are simply checks that people draw on a bank where they have no account.

Does the leper *choose* to be a leper, to be isolated and ostracized and alone, all the time? Do you think all he has to do is make *choices* and resolutions to improve his circumstances?

It's not just lepers. How many of you are in situations you did not choose, situations that defy your resolutions? Ranging perhaps from emotional disorders to toxic family dysfunction to mountains of debt to chronic medical conditions to addictions to feeling trapped in a marriage—these are situations you would never have chosen for yourself.

The leper knew that ultimately when it came to his condition, that it was Jesus' choice that mattered, not his own—"If *you* choose," the leper said to Jesus, "*You* can make me clean."

"If you choose" can also be translated "if you are willing" or… "if you want to." How does Jesus respond? Mark writes that Jesus was "moved with pity."

The phrase "moved with pity" can also be also translated "moved with compassion." Compassion was always the starting point of Jesus' ministry. The Bible tells us: "When (Jesus) saw the crowds, he had compassion for them, because they were harassed and helpless, like sheep without a shepherd" (Matthew 9:36).

Jesus was moved with pity, moved with compassion for the leper, and defying the ceremonial and ritual law of the Old Testament, which forbade anyone from touching a leper lest they be defiled, Jesus "stretched out his hand and touched (the leper)"—perhaps the first time the leper had been touched in years.

And Jesus looked the leper in the eye and said, "I do choose. Be made clean!" In touching the leper Jesus incurred defilement according to Mosaic Law, but in spite of the finger-wagging of the self-righteous religious leaders—as scholar Walter Wessel put it, "(Jesus) boldly placed love and compassion over ritual and regulation."

And Jesus' compassionate touch healed the leper. Mark tells us that "immediately the leprosy left him, and he was made clean."

Have you ever received a compassionate hug that brought you comfort and healing? It's what can happen when a dad hugs his sobbing daughter who's been used and dropped by a boyfriend, or when friends who have had a massive falling out are reconciled and embrace. It's what happens when someone knows all about you—your successes, failures, neuroses, all of it—and not only still loves you but still *likes* you too, and gives you a hug to prove it.

That kind of compassionate touch *heals.*

Think about your life for a moment. In the same way lepers in Jesus' day had to identify themselves as unclean so that people would stay away from them, our hearts feel unclean, and therefore we think God wants nothing to do with us. We feel unclean in our hearts for things we have done, things that were entirely their fault; we feel unclean in our hearts because of things that were done to us, things that were not our fault at all. For many, it's a combination of the two.

And this sense of self-reproach can blanket us with shame, and the sense that God could never love someone like us, never ever. This sense of self-reproach is not something people choose for themselves, and it in itself defies any resolutions to choose to get over it.

The only thing that can make people feel clean again, in their hearts, is the grace of God, the grace Jesus gives the leper.

I heard it preached once that we often define ourselves either by what has been done *by* us or by what has been done *to* us. But because of the grace of God in Jesus Christ, we are defined neither by what has been done *by* us nor *to* us; rather, we are defined by what has been done *for* us...in Jesus' death on the cross. In his death on the cross Jesus shed his blood *for* us, we have been made clean—and *that* is what defines us.

In his death on the cross covered all the wrong things that have been done *by* you or *to* you. It was not your choice; it was his choice. God chooses to make you clean because he chooses to. God's grace can take the ugly things in your life and make something beautiful.

A couple weeks ago I watched the film, *500 Days of Summer* (2009), about a young man named Tom (Joseph Gordon-Levitt) and his 500-day relationship with a girl named Summer (Zooey Deschanel). Near the end of the film Summer breaks up with Tom, but Tom is still in love with her.

Later Summer invites Tom to a party she's hosting. As Tom arrives at her party the movie then splits into two sections— the left-half is subtitled "Expectations" and the right-half subtitled "Reality"—and simultaneously you watch both scenarios played out.

On the "Expectations" half, you see Tom being greeted affectionately at the door by Summer; he gives her a gift for which she is excessively grateful. The rest of the sequence shows Tom and Summer talking, flirting, and eventually kissing as they rekindle their relationship. This is what Tom's expecting and hoping for. On the "Reality" half you see Tom being greeted politely but distantly by Summer, who smiles at the gift but is not at all touched by it. The rest of the sequence shows Tom, nursing a drink and awkwardly trying to engage with various people in conversation, while Summer all but ignores him. Then, as he sees Summer showing off a ring, he realizes that she's engaged to another man, and that the party she had invited him to was actually her *engagement* party. Obviously, Tom is devastated and quickly departs. As he leaves the party the "Reality" half of the movie slowly expands until it covers the entire screen, literally erasing Tom's "Expectations."

It is a brilliant piece of film-making, and it resonates because, how often in your life has reality slowly covered your better expectations, until your expectations and hopes are no longer even on the screen?

The good news of the Gospel is that this is all reversed, that God's grace—which eventually is better than anything you could have expected or hoped for— is the ultimate reality in your life, not your expectations.

That is what the leper encountered from Jesus, who was moved with pity and compassion, and whose touch healed him and made him clean.

And it's the same for you.

The good news of the Gospel is that if you feel unclean and your *expectations* from God are wrath and judgment, the *reality* is that God gives you grace instead, grace that makes you clean. God has always been and is now moved with pity and compassion for you, because he has chosen to. And in time the reality of God's grace will cover everything in your life, the entire screen.

Back to *500 Days of Summer* for a moment... the movie doesn't end with Tom leaving Summer's engagement party (it wouldn't be much of a rom-com if it did). At the very end of the film he meets a beautiful girl at a job interview. She smiles at him and introduces herself, "Hi, my name is... *Autumn"*—literally a new season for Tom.

So regardless of what kind of Valentine's Day you have this year, be encouraged, because the grace of God in Jesus Christ is a Valentine for every kid in the class, including you, and there are no strings attached.

Amen.

GOD SENT HIS SON TO SAVE THE WORLD
Rip Tides, Friendship Bracelets, and Nicodemus' Gospel Train

For God so loved the world that he gave his only Son, so that everyone who believes in him may not perish but may have eternal life. Indeed, God did not send the Son into the world to condemn the world, but in order that the world might be saved through him (John 3:16-17).

In the Name of the Father, Son, and Holy Spirit.

It's the summer of 1977. You're eight years old, at the beach for the very first time. The beach is crazy crowded, umbrellas of every color dot the shore, multiple radios are playing songs by Fleetwood Mac, The Eagles, or K.C. and the Sunshine Band, the salty air is pungent with the smell of sunscreen. Your dad has rented a raft—navy blue in the middle, bright yellow on the ends—and you spend all day long riding the waves in again and again, even surviving a jellyfish sting.

The next day you're back at the beach, now a seasoned veteran of riding the waves. Dripping with confidence you start to venture a little farther out each time...until one time out of nowhere a riptide whooshes you farther out than you ever wanted to go. You try and try to paddle back to shore, but the tide continues to take you farther out. Your confidence has been replaced by fear.

You see a lifeguard standing on his tall wooden white chair, surrounded by his bikini-clad groupies, blowing his whistle and waving you back in, but you can't come back in, no matter how hard you try—the tide is just too strong. You slide off the raft and grab onto the cord and begin doggy-paddling, but then you have images of the movie *Jaws* in your mind, and you remember what happened to the boy who was riding a raft just like the one you're riding, so you climb back on your raft... and you start crying.

The lifeguard is still standing, blowing the whistle, and waving you in, but it doesn't matter, because there's nothing you can do.

Finally, you see a different lifeguard swimming toward you. As he gets near, you slide off the raft again and begin dog-paddling because you want to "do your part." When he arrives, slightly out of breath, he grins and says two sentences you'll never forget, "It's going to be okay. I've got you."

He brings you safely to shore and you make sure to wipe your eyes because you don't want anyone to know you've been crying. After you wade through the surf the lifeguard ruffles your hair and smiles, "Enjoy the rest of your day." You drag your raft back to your family's beach umbrella, utterly relieved. You have been saved, and K. C. and the Sunshine Band have never sounded so good...

In today's Gospel lesson we see the heart of the Gospel—that Jesus came to *save* us.

Jesus is talking with a Pharisee named Nicodemus, who wanted to talk with Jesus at night because he didn't want any of his Pharisee friends to see him. During their conversation Jesus clearly states the reason why he came to earth:

> God so loved the world that he gave his only Son, so that everyone who believes in him may not perish but may have eternal life. Indeed, God did not send the Son into the world to condemn the world, but in order that the world might be saved through him (John 3:16-17).

That is the Gospel—God loves you and sent Jesus to save you.

Do you know how many verses there are in the Bible? I'm *sure* you were wondering that on the way to church today: 31,101. Out of these 31,101 verses perhaps the most famous of all is John 3:16. John 3:16 is everywhere—bumper stickers, t-shirts, signs held by the guy with the rainbow-colored afro wig at football games, on the black under the eyes of QB Tim Tebow.

Because of its familiarity, John 3:16 is often dismissed as cliché. It's like the song you've heard so many times on the radio that you—like it or not—surf the dial for something new. But John 3:16, along with verse 17, captures the heart of the Gospel—it is the song that we must hear again and again. Jesus tells Nicodemus that God loves everyone in the whole world. Everyone.

One of my favorite Anglican scholars, the late Leon Morris, describes this love of God for everyone in the world:

> It is a distinctively Christian idea that God's love is wide enough to embrace all people. His love is not confined to any national group or spiritual elite. It is a love that proceeds from the fact that he is love (I John 4:8, 16). It is his nature to love. He loves people because he is the kind of God he is...in recent times some scholars have argued that John sees God's love as only for believers, but here it is plain that God loves 'the world' (*The Gospel According to John*, 203).

Recently Bruce Springsteen released a new album, *Wrecking Ball*, and it includes a new version of his powerful song, "Land of Hope and Dreams." Several years ago I saw Springsteen and the E Street Band play this song live, and it felt like a revival was taking place as he sang about the train of salvation:

> This train carries saints and sinners
> This train carries losers and winners
> This train carries whores and gamblers
> This train carries lost souls
> This train carries broken hearted
> Thieves and sweet souls departed
> This train carries fools and kings...
> All aboard.

As they neared the end of this song the E Street Band then shifted into a rendition of Curtis Mayfield's classic song, "People Get Ready":

> People get ready there's a train comin'
> You don't need no baggage, just get on board
> All you need is faith to hear the diesels hummin'
> You don't need no ticket, you just thank the Lord

That's pure Gospel, that we don't need to bring any supplemental baggage with us to board God's salvation train, that we don't even need a ticket, because Jesus has already purchased the ticket for every person in the world, that we simply thank the Lord—it's straight-up, high octane Gospel.

"For God so loved the *world*..." Jesus tells Nicodemus.

In his conversation with Nicodemus Jesus also references an event from the Old Testament, recorded in the Book of Numbers. While Israel was in the wilderness they found themselves attacked by poisonous serpents, and many of them died. They asked Moses to pray that the Lord would take away the serpents.

The Lord responded to Moses' prayer with a rather curious command: "Make a poisonous serpent, and set it on a pole; and everyone who is bitten shall look at it and live." It's curious because Moses was asked to make an image of the very thing that was literally killing the Israelites. And yet Moses did exactly that—he made a bronze serpent and lifted it up on a pole and the writer of Numbers tells us that, "Whenever a serpent bit someone, that person would look at the serpent of bronze and live" (Numbers 21:7-9).

And Jesus tells Nicodemus, "Just as Moses lifted up the serpent in the wilderness, so must the Son of Man be lifted up, that whoever believes in him may have eternal life" (John 3:15). The very thing that literally kills Jesus, crucifixion, has become for Christians the sign of life, *eternal* life.

In his masterful book, *The Cross of Christ*, Stott describes this:

> A universally acceptable Christian emblem would obviously need to speak of Jesus Christ, but there was a wide range of possibilities. Christians might have chosen the manger in which the baby Jesus was laid, or the carpenter's bench at which he

worked... or the boat from which he taught the crowds in Galilee, or the apron he wore when washing the apostles' feet... Then there was the stone which, having been rolled from the mouth of the tomb, would have proclaimed his resurrection... But the chosen symbol came to be a simple cross...(Christians) wished to commemorate as central to their understanding of Jesus neither his birth nor his youth, neither his teaching nor his service, neither his resurrection nor his reign... but his death, his crucifixion.

In the same way the sign of death in the wilderness—a serpent—was a symbol of healing for the Israelites who had been bitten, the sign of death—the cross—became a symbol of life for Christians. This is because in his death on the cross Jesus saved the world, just as he told Nicodemus: "God did not send the Son into the world to condemn the world, but in order that the world might be *saved* through him."

Jesus did not come to condemn the world, because due to sin the world was already condemned.

Let me ask you a question... what if the lifeguard had swum out to me when I was drifting out to sea just to let me know I was in trouble and that I really should swim back to shore, and then had turned around and swam back to shore without me? It sounds absurd, but that is exactly what happens when a lot of people go to church. Instead of walking out feeling *relief* because they have heard the Gospel of God's grace and forgiveness, they walk out feeling *more* condemned than they felt when they walked into church in the first place.

The reason the Gospel is good news for everyone is because when Jesus died on the cross he atoned for all the sin of the *whole world*, all of it. That is why Thomas Cranmer—the leading figure of the English Reformation—emphasized this in his 1549 Eucharistic prayer, as he wrote that Jesus "made (on the cross), by his one oblation of himself once offered, a full, perfect, and sufficient sacrifice, oblation, and satisfaction, for the sins of the *whole world*" *(BCP, 334)*.

And in Article 31 of the Thirty-nine Articles—the classic distillation of the theology of the English Reformation, which Cranmer also helped write—there is again emphasis on Jesus' death on the cross atoning for the sin of the *whole world*:

> The Offering of Christ once made is that perfect redemption, propitiation, and satisfaction, for all the sins of the *whole world*, both original and actual; and there is none other satisfaction for sin, but that alone *(BCP, 974)*.

Notice that the phrase "whole world" is used in each of these places. Why was Cranmer being so redundant? Because it sounds too good to be true, to think that Jesus' death on the cross really cleanses all of us from each and every sin, that there are no exceptions, that there is nothing we can do to "do our part"—it sounds too good to be true. But it is true— that's why it's such good news.

The reality is that people often feel condemned, and they need to be reminded of what Jesus told Nicodemus, that "God did not send the Son into the world to condemn the world, but in order that the world might be saved through him."

The reality is that people, even in the church... *especially* in the church, still often feel condemned by others, or condemned by themselves, for the sin in their lives.

But our hope is that, even if others condemn you or even if you condemn yourself, God has *not* condemned you, because Jesus stood already condemned in your place. The good news of the Gospel is that, as Paul wrote to the Romans, "There is therefore now *no condemnation* for those who are in Christ Jesus" (Romans 8:1).

So what happened to Nicodemus after his conversation with Jesus?

John mentions Nicodemus twice more in his account of the Gospel. Toward the end of the seventh chapter the Pharisees are plotting how they can destroy the ministry of Jesus and Nicodemus speaks up on Jesus' behalf, "Our law does not judge people without first giving them a hearing to find out what they are doing, does it?" (John 7:50). Later Nicodemus appears one more time...after—like the bronze serpent in the wilderness—Jesus was lifted up on the cross, after Jesus was condemned in our place. Listen to what Nicodemus does:

> After these things, Joseph of Arimathea, who was a disciple of Jesus, though a secret one because of his fear of the Jews, asked Pilate to let him take away the body of Jesus. Pilate gave him permission; so he came and removed his body. Nicodemus, who had at first come to Jesus by night, also came, bringing a mixture of myrrh and aloes, weighing about a hundred pounds. They took the body of Jesus and wrapped it with the spices in linen cloths, according to the burial custom of the Jews (John 19:38-40).

Nicodemus the Pharisee, in his Pharisee robes, carried a hundred pounds of myrrh and aloes to the cross and, in spite of ritually defiling himself by touching a corpse, helped Joseph of Arimathea take Jesus' body from the cross and embalm it. Apparently the conversation with Jesus made quite the impact on Nicodemus.

One more image... I recently spent a week in Honduras on a mission trip with others from Christ Church as well as members of St. James' Episcopal Church, Richmond. Among the many things we did was spend time with the girls of Our Little Roses, a home for girls ranging from 2 to 17 years old who need a safe place to live. During our last evening there most of our group was playing soccer with the girls, but I was out of gas. Instead I just sat, holding yarn for a little girl named Jasupa, as she wove one friendship bracelet after another. After finishing each friendship bracelet she would wander off and tie it around someone's wrist, and then return to me and begin weaving another one. After completing her fifth and final friendship bracelet, instead of wandering off, she tied it around my wrist, smiled, and said, "Thank you!" Then she skipped away to play with the other kids.

I've got that friendship bracelet on right now—it fits perfectly—a friendship bracelet I have no clue how to weave. Jasupa wove it for me because she wanted to; all I did was receive it.

The good news of the Gospel is that Jesus is the Friend of Sinners, that Jesus swam out to all of you who have been carried off by the tide of sin and circumstances, to save you, to say to you, "It's going to be okay. I've got you." No dog-paddling needed.

The good news of the Gospel is that God loves the *whole world* and that Jesus was already condemned for all the sins of the *whole world*, including yours and mine, and that's why "there is now no condemnation for those who are in Christ Jesus."

And Jesus has saved you; he has woven a friendship bracelet of love and mercy and tied it on your wrist because he is the *Friend* of Sinners—and the friendship bracelet God has made you fits perfectly.

Amen.

SEE WHAT LOVE THE FATHER HAS GIVEN US
Coors Light and the Ministry of Substitution

See what love the Father has given us, that we should be called children of God; and that is what we are (1 John 3:1).

In the Name of the Father, Son, and Holy Spirit.

One summer Saturday morning about nine years ago I was working in the front yard, as were several of our neighbors. We had just moved to Charlottesville, and our neighbors were still sizing us up. They had heard I was a priest and my family kind of felt under a microscope. My four-year old son Paul was playing in the yard and he asked me if he could have a Diet Coke. "Sure," I replied. He went to the kitchen and, out of the corner of my eye, I saw him come back out the front door and sit on the front step, but I wasn't really paying attention.

A few minutes later he said, "Dad, this tastes weird." I didn't bother looking up, just told him it was fine and kept working. A few minutes later Paul continued, "Dad, this Diet Coke tastes really yucky." I looked over and saw that it wasn't Diet Coke he was drinking...it was Coors Light. I laughed and told him, "That's not Diet Coke, son. That's beer." I remember wondering what the neighbors were thinking as they watched their new priest-neighbor's four-year-old son pounding beer on the front porch. Of course the upside is that they probably weren't surprised—after all they knew we were Episcopalians.

We don't always pay close attention to our kids—that's the bad news. The good news is that God always pays close attention to us, his children, and that God loves his children more than we could ever know.

This morning I'm preaching on just one verse from 1 John wherein he writes, "See what love the Father has given us, that we should be called children of God" (3:1).

The youngest of Jesus' twelve disciples, John was perhaps a teenager during Jesus' earthly life. He outlived all the other disciples, all of whom were martyred, except of course Judas. In fact, John lived to be quite old and in his last years he wrote five books included in the New Testament. Toward the end of his life John became so infirm that he was literally carried to various churches, where he would always address his fellow believers as "little children." John would always preach about the same thing: God's love. This is the case with his New Testament writings as well. Love is the main theme of John's writings.

It is John who recorded Jesus' words to Nicodemus, "For God so loved the world that he gave his only Son..." (John

3:16). It was John who recorded Jesus' words at the Last Supper, "Just as I have loved you, you also should love one another" (John 13:34). It was John who wrote, "In this is love, not that we loved God but that he loved us and sent his Son to be the atoning sacrifice for our sins" (1 John 4:10). And it was John who wrote simply, "God is love" (1 John 4:8 and 16).

Several years ago a crabby older man wanted to take me to lunch. I knew something was up, but I accepted his invitation anyway. (Perhaps you know the joy of being invited to *that* kind of lunch.) We met at a restaurant and, after the initial small talk, the axe fell and he unloaded on me, "Why do you always preach about God's love? People need to hear about God's judgment and wrath. People need to straighten out their lives. People need more than touchy-feely sermons— they need 'balanced' preaching." Crabbiness in overdrive, he was on a roll. It was a delightful meal. I listened to him, but I disagreed with him. I still do. The heart of the Gospel is God's love, and God's love is anything but "balanced."

"Balanced" preaching has nothing to do with the Gospel. People are unable to "straighten out" their lives, and the Gospel is that God takes our place, atones by *substitution*. The Bible is explicitly clear that love and compassion, Jesus' entire ministry, was entirely one-sided. Those who really think the Gospel is about straightening out your life can become—well, crabby—and it can ruin an otherwise perfect lunch.

The heart of Gospel is the love of God in Jesus Christ—a love that transcends all bounds, a love that is unconditional, a love that cannot be measured or bullet-pointed in a dry theological textbook—a love for sinners whose lives are a complete train wreck—a love with no ulterior motives, no strings attached, no catch—a love that sounds too good to be true and yet is true—a love that gives hope to the hopeless— a love that brings relief and comfort to the beat-up, the bedraggled, and the burned-out—a love that makes all things new.

The love of God is too great for us to even begin to comprehend. Writing from prison to the Christians at Ephesus, Paul put it this way, "I pray that you may have the power to comprehend, with all the saints, what is the breadth and length and height and depth, and to know the love of Christ that surpasses knowledge" (Ephesians 3:18-19). Paul is praying that the Ephesians can know something they'll never *begin* to know fully.

The love of God in Jesus Christ is the heart of the Gospel—and John never got over it. For John the love of God is always front and center. And it was this love that John wrote about in today's lesson—"See what love the Father has given us that we should be called children of God."

When it comes to loving and paying attention to their kids, earthly parents often fall short, no matter how hard they try. That's why it's so important to teach kids about forgiveness—as I saw on a poster recently—"Teach every child you meet the importance of forgiveness. It's our only hope of surviving their wrath once they realize just how badly we've messed things up for them."

In the mid-fifties there was a sixth-grader who lived in Queens, New York City and whose dad was a college professor. He became obsessed with rock 'n' roll. Unlike many parents, who scoffed at the interests of their awkward middle school kids, this boy's dad supported him. The boy wrote a song called, "The Girl for Me," and his dad, who often worked until late at night, still found the time to write out the words and music for his son and his friend to use as they sang it. It became quite a hit at the middle school dances.

Meanwhile there was another sixth grader who lived in Minnesota and whose dad sold appliances and furniture. He too became obsessed with rock 'n' roll and so his dad built a large antenna and mounted it on the roof of the family home so his son could hear radio stations from all over. He especially liked the blues of the Deep South. He too began to write songs and play at school dances.

The boy from Queens was Paul Simon and his friend, of course, was Art Garfunkel. The boy from Minnesota was Robert Zimmerman, who later changed his name to Bob Dylan.
Both Paul Simon and Bob Dylan had dads who supported their sons in just the right way at just the right time—and certainly their paying attention to their sons has had quite the ripple effect.

In the summer of 1999 Paul Simon and Bob Dylan went on tour together. One of my best friends and I went to the concert they did in Raleigh, North Carolina. They both played individual sets, as well as a joint set. I'll never forget that concert. The last song they played together during their joint set was Paul Simon's masterful "The Sound of Silence." A hush fell over the crowd as these two rock 'n' roll icons began, "Hello darkness my old friend, I've come to talk with you again…"

Even if you have supportive parents you can still go through times when you feel alone in the darkness, times when God is silent, when you wonder if your Heavenly Father is paying any attention to your life at all.

The good news of the Gospel is that God is paying close attention to you because he loves you and cares about every detail in your life, even if he is silent.

Sometime ago a friend of mine died after several years of battling a degenerative disease. He was an amazing husband and dad, and loved by many in the community. One of his sons was a lacrosse prodigy, a prolific scorer who went on to play in college. My friend went to every one of his son's lacrosse games, even as the disease progressed and his health regressed. Even after he lost his ability to walk and talk his loving wife still took him to each of their son's lacrosse games.

And after each game his son would walk over to his dad, now silently watching from a wheelchair, and do you know what his dad would do? He would smile and somehow manage to hold up the same number of fingers as the number of goals he had just seen his son score. He wanted his son to know that even though he could no longer walk or talk, he still loved him, he was still proud of him, he was still fully aware of what was going on in his life.

And even if God is silent, he still loves you...and he is still fully aware of every detail in your life. While Scripture is silent about God keeping tally of how many goals you've scored, the Bible does tell us God knows the number of hairs on your head—and the Bible does tell us that God holds every one of your tears in a jar—for some of you, right now, it's a really big jar, but never too big for God.

Maybe there have been times when you really felt loved by God, times when you really knew he was paying attention and moving in your life. However, for many people that tends to be the exception rather than the rule.

As finite human beings we are confined to time, matter, and space. We can't go forward in time to do or undo things we wish we could. We can't change into something that we aren't. We can't be in two places at once. But God is beyond time, matter, and space. He pays attention to you and loves you during every moment of your life—your first breath, first birthday, first ice cream cone—your first scraped knee, first kiss, first broken heart—your proudest moments and most embarrassing moments—your moments of youthful idealism, middle-aged cynicism, and elderly perspective. From the moment you are helpless at your birth to the moment when you are helpless at your death, God loves you and is attentive to your every need.

And when God is silent, when we wonder if God really loves us, if God is really paying attention to us, we can always look back to the ultimate proof of God's love: Jesus' death on the cross for us. When Jesus is dying on the cross and he cries out in dereliction "My God, my God, why have you forsaken me?" God the Father is silent. And yet of course Jesus' Heavenly Father loves him and is paying attention, and of course his heart is breaking too. Any of you who have watched your children suffer in a hospital, be made fun of or bullied because of something they can't help, know that there's nothing worse.

The longtime Yale professor and theologian Nicholas Wolterstorff lost his twenty-five year old son Eric in a mountain climbing accident. In his moving book, *Lament for a Son*, he wrote this about his son's funeral:

> I buried myself that warm June day. It was me those gardeners lowered on squeaking straps into that hot dry hole, curious neighborhood children looking down in at me, everyone stilled, wind rustling the oaks. It was me over whom we slid that heavy slab, more than I can lift. It was me on whom we shoveled dirt. It was me we left behind (42).

And that is what happens on Good Friday—God the Father's heart breaks as he watches his only beloved Son die at the hands of sinners. And yet even though God the Father is silent as Jesus is dying on the cross, Jesus' final words attest that God the Father still loves him and is paying attention. Otherwise Jesus does not gasp, "Father, into your hands I commit my spirit."

And John is one of Jesus' twelve disciples who sees it all happen. He watches Jesus suffer. John stands next to Mary as she weeps. John listens to the labored breathing of Jesus, until his breathing stops. And John stays at the cross for awhile after that and watches as the Roman soldier spears Jesus in the side to confirm his death. John sees the fount of Jesus' blood pour onto the dusty ground.

In other words, John personally witnesses the full extent of God's love for His children—"See what love the Father has given us."

And so it's no wonder John never got over the love of God. No wonder he never stopped preaching about the love of God. No wonder that for John the love of God was front and center. Many years after Jesus' death John wrote this in the prologue of his account of the gospel: "To all who received (Jesus), who believed in his name, he gave power to become children of God" (John 1:12).

And that is our response to the unbalanced love of God—to believe and receive. The final song on Bob Dylan's 1979 album *Slow Train Coming* is about Jesus' Second Coming and is entitled "When He Returns." In the final verse he shows us what it can look like to believe and receive the love of God in Jesus Christ:

> Surrender your crown on this blood-stained ground, take off your mask
> He sees your deeds, he knows your needs even before you ask
> How long can you falsify and deny what is real?
> How long can you hate yourself for the weakness you conceal?
> Of every earthly plan that be known to man, he is unconcerned
> He's got plans of his own to set up his throne
> When he returns

And when Jesus, the King of Love, returns he will indeed set up his throne, his throne of love, or what Scripture calls his throne of grace.

We will join the millions upon millions of our brothers and sisters in Christ as we experience firsthand the joy of the unbalanced, immeasurable love of God—and we will experience to the fullest extent the truth of John's words: "See what love the Father has given us that we should be called children of God, and that is what we are."

Amen.

THE VALLEY OF THE SHADOW OF DEATH
Independence, Wilderness, and Our Hour of Darkness

*Though I walk through the valley of the shadow
of death,
I shall fear no evil;
for you are with me;
your rod and your staff, they comfort me (Psalm
23:4, BCP 613).*

In the Name of the Father, Son, and Holy Spirit.

It's a Friday night in April 1994 and your wife has just given birth to a beautiful baby girl, an adorable seven-pound blessing from God. You're so happy that you're literally laughing and crying at the same time—and you notice that she has your eyes. You start phoning your family and friends to share the good news.

After a while, however, the joy quickly turns awry as you notice the doctors and nurses glancing at each other with concern. "What's wrong?" you ask them. "We're concerned about her breathing," they respond, as they take her from the delivery room. Later that night they tell you they're rushing her in an ambulance to Children's Hospital in Washington D.C. You're denied permission to ride in the ambulance and so you kiss your sobbing wife goodbye and get in your Toyota.

It's pouring rain. As you're driving you're praying and crying and cursing and then telling God you're sorry for cursing and then you pray and cry and curse some more. You wish you had windshield wipers for your eyes.

It's about 3:30 in the morning when you arrive at Children's Hospital and the security guard tells you how to get to the NICU. You step off the elevator, enter the unit and ask a nurse for help. Within a few minutes a doctor emerges and escorts you into a small waiting room. She's compassionate, kind and soft-spoken, but she asks you to sit down. You know that's never a good sign.

She tells you that your daughter has severe Respiratory Distress Syndrome, and that she will probably not survive— and that if she somehow does survive she will spend months in the hospital and will most likely have a host of life-long mental and physical problems. It's too much to take in. As you struggle without success to maintain your composure you ask if you can see her.

You don a light blue protective gown and mask and latex gloves, and are led into the NICU. In the back section where the most critically ill babies are you find your new baby girl. She's on her back, head to the side, a tube running down her throat and into her tiny struggling lungs, monitors attached to her chest and head, various lines attached to veins in her arms, head, and even her belly-button. Her brow is furrowed and you see an intense look in her brown eyes. You spread your fingers apart and try to avoid the monitors and lines as you gently place your fingertips on her little body, which is vibrating like a washing machine because the oxygen pump is turned all the way up.

You're in the valley of the shadow of death and you're more scared and more helpless and more out of control than you have ever been in your life and you do the only thing you can do… you pray, you ask God to please help.

Apparently God does help because your baby girl not only survives but goes on to lead a healthy and happy childhood. When you watch her play sports you can still occasionally glimpse the same intensity in her furrowed brow. Each year on her birthday you thank God anew and give her an extra long hug because you never forget how it felt to be in the valley of the shadow of death. The years fly by and all of the sudden it's the morning of her eighteenth birthday and you're driving to worship at Christ Episcopal Church.

Today is the fourth Sunday of Easter, Good Shepherd Sunday. Each year on this Sunday we are reminded that Jesus is the Good Shepherd who is always with us—even in the valley of the shadow of death. With that in mind today I'm preaching from the fourth verse of Psalm 23, a psalm written by David.

Knowing about the circumstances during which something was written can help us appreciate it more. For example, knowing Beethoven was deaf when he composed his *Ninth Symphony* or knowing Harper Lee wrote *To Kill a Mockingbird* during the early stages of the Civil Rights Movement can help us appreciate those masterpieces even more. This is certainly the case with Psalm 23.

Psalm 23 was not written during a peaceful time in King David's life, when everything was going well and everyone liked him and it was a perfect sunny day and he was lounging about with a harp watching sheep as they idyllically grazed. King David wrote Psalm 23 in the latter years of his life and in the midst of extreme stress.

The cause of this extreme stress was family dysfunction—some things never change. David has several wives and multiple children and therefore multiplied family dysfunction as well. By one wife he has a son named Absalom and a daughter named Tamar. By another wife he has a son named Amnon. Amnon violates Tamar, and Tamar's brother Absalom is furious. Absalom doesn't speak to Amnon for two years, and then succeeds in his conspiracy to have him killed while inebriated at a party. Absalom flees Jerusalem and stays away for three years, after which he returns and wants to be reconciled with his father, but his father refuses to see him for another two years. Finally Absalom is allowed to see his father, who kisses him.

It appears that Absalom and his father David are now reconciled, but it's a front. For the next four years Absalom conspires against David and wins over the hearts of the military and civil leaders of Israel. He then goes to Hebron and, while there, the nation of Israel proclaims Absalom as king. Word comes to David that Absalom and the armies of Israel are heading to Jerusalem to kill him, so David, the great king of Israel, flees Jerusalem with his servants. As he flees, some people along the road curse him and throw stones at him.

When Absalom arrives at Jerusalem he moves into the palace vacated by David—and to add insult to injury, he pitches a tent on the roof of the palace where he sleeps with his father David's concubines for all to see.

Later Absalom leads an army to seek out his father David and kill him—but in the meantime many Israelites have rallied behind David in the wilderness. When it comes time for battle David orders his generals, "Deal gently for my sake with the young man Absalom." But instead, as they defeated all who had revolted against him, they violently kill Absalom. When David received news of Absalom's death, he wept and cried out again and again, "O my son, Absalom, my son, my son Absalom! Would I had died instead of you, O Absalom, my son, my son!" (2 Samuel 13-18).

It was while the humiliated King David was in the wilderness fleeing his son Absalom that he wrote Psalm 23.

Psalm 23 is one of the best known and best loved passages of the Bible. One could preach a whole series of sermons on each verse, sermons about how God makes us lie down in green pastures or leads us beside still waters or revives our souls or guides us along the right paths. But today I am going to focus on verse four, which assures us that the Lord is our shepherd even in the valley of the shadow of death.

Psalm 23 was written to comfort and encourage individuals who are in the wilderness. Both intentional, literal outings to the wilderness and unintentional, figurative wilderness seasons in your life can be scary.

One of my favorite seminary professors was Tim Laniak, without question one of the smartest people I know. We still keep in touch. He is also compassionate. One semester I had fallen way behind in my Hebrew studies and completely bombed a quiz. When I received my quiz back Tim had wryly written, "Definitely not a keeper," next to the low score, and he mercifully dropped the grade.

While on sabbatical Tim spent a year in the Middle East living in the wilderness with Bedouin shepherds, and he wrote a devotional book based on his experiences entitled *While Shepherds Watch Their Flocks*. Listen to how Tim describes the effect the wilderness has on people:

> Deserts bring people quickly to the end of their self-sufficiency and independence… Our lives can become a wilderness when experiences expose our frail and tenuous existence. Episodes of bewilderment, abandonment, and inner terror reveal our soul's restless cravings and fundamental neediness. In the wilderness we can lose our bearings (24-25).

Sometimes the wilderness can be very dark. In verse four of Psalm 23 we read, "Though I walk through the valley of the shadow of death, I shall fear no evil; for you are with me." The phrase "shadow of death" is actually a mild translation. David is not referring to passing shadows or twilight; he is referring to total darkness.

A number of years ago I led an outdoor adventure camp for about 30 high school students. We spent the week mountain biking, rock climbing, whitewater rafting, hiking, and caving—or spelunking. At one point, while spelunking, we reached a place deep inside a mountain. Our guide asked all of us to turn our flashlights and helmet lights off. We did, and within seconds it was absolutely pitch dark. You literally could not even see your hand in front of you. Talk about unnerving. Of course, within a few seconds the kids all started making weird noises and off-color remarks, and so we turned our lights back on and continued, but I'll never forget how that absolute darkness felt.

And in every one of our lives we experience moments or seasons of absolute darkness. No one is immune. The 16th century Spanish mystic St. John of the Cross famously referred to this kind of experience as a "dark night of the soul." The brilliant 20th century poet T. S. Eliot describes this in his *Four Quartets*:

> O dark dark dark. They all go into the dark,

The vacant interstellar spaces, the vacant into the
    vacant,
The captains, merchant bankers, eminent men of
    letters,
The generous patrons of art, the statesmen and the
    rulers,
Distinguished civil servants, chairmen of many
    committees,
Industrial lords and petty contractors, all go into the
    dark.

On one level this darkness is the darkness of death; on another level it is the figurative darkness during which you cannot see any direction at all.

But the good news is you're not alone in the darkness. The Lord is right there with you, and that means you don't have to be afraid—"Though I walk through the valley of the shadow of death, I shall fear no evil; for you are with me." Even if you are afraid of the dark, God is not, and he is still with you.

One of my favorite writers is Cormac McCarthy. His Pulitzer Prize winning novel *The Road* is about a father and son trying to survive in a post-apocalyptic nightmare of a world. At one point in the story after resting for awhile one afternoon the father decides they need to continue walking down the road:

> We're okay, [the father] said. Come on.
> [His son asked,] Is the dark going to catch
> us?
> I don't know.
> It is, isn't it?
> Come on. We'll hurry.
> The dark did catch them. By the time they
> reached the headland path it was too dark to
> see anything. They stood in the wind from off
> the sea with the grass hissing all about them,

the boy holding his hand. We just have to
keep going, the man said. Come on.
I can't see [the boy said].
I know. We'll just take it one step at a time.
Okay.
Don't let go.
Okay.
No matter what.
No matter what (233).

The Lord your Shepherd is with you no matter what. And
even if you let go of his hand, he never lets go of yours. The
Lord is your Shepherd, especially in the valley of the shadow
of death.

In the New Testament we see an even deeper meaning for
Psalm 23. In the Gospel According to John, Jesus identifies
himself as the Good Shepherd: "I am the Good Shepherd. The
Good Shepherd lays down his life for the sheep" (10:11). Jesus
allows the darkness to catch him. In his suffering and death
Jesus entered into the "dark dark dark" of human depravity
and sin, and bore the price of that sin, death, in our place.

The Roman soldiers were not gentle with Jesus as they
violently killed him, and as he died perhaps God the Father
echoed King David: "O my son, Jesus, my son, my son Jesus!
Would I had died instead of you, O Jesus, my son, my son!"

On the cross Jesus the Good Shepherd did what he said he
would do, he laid down his life for the sheep, including you.
He not only dropped all the lowest grades in your life, he
dropped *all* the grades in your life. On the cross Jesus the
Good Shepherd took the place of the lost and sinful sheep,
and became a lamb, the Lamb of God who takes away the sin
of the world. The 17th century hymnist Johann Heermann
expressed it this way:

Lo, the Good Shepherd for the sheep is offered;
the slave hath sinned and the Son hath suffered

For our atonement while we nothing heeded
God interceded (158, *1982 Episcopal Hymnal*).

In the mid-fifties a fourteen-year old boy lost his mother to cancer. The combination of his mother's death and his father's grief rattled him to the core. About twelve years later he had a dream one night in which his mother appeared to him and comforted him with the words, "It will be all right, just let it be." The boy was Paul McCartney, his mother's name was Mary, and the song this dream inspired is the Beatles classic, "Let It Be," a song that resonates on a deep level with people who feel like they are in the dark:

> When I find myself in times of trouble
> Mother Mary comes to me
> Speaking words of wisdom
> Let it be
>
> And in my hour of darkness
> She is standing right in front of me
> Speaking words of wisdom
> Let it be

So today if you are in one way or another in the valley of the shadow of death, disoriented in the wilderness and at the end of your self-sufficiency and independence, perhaps more scared and more helpless and more out of control than you have ever been before, be encouraged.

The Lord is still your Shepherd who will always be with you, especially in your hour of darkness. No matter what.

And at the end of Psalm 23 we see that one day the darkness will be over, and you will find yourself in the house of the Good Shepherd who will stand right in front of you and wipe every tear from your eyes, and you "will dwell in the house of the Lord forever."

Amen.

NO GREATER LOVE
Letting a Mother off the Hook

*"No one has greater love than this, to lay down
one's life for one's friends" (John 15:13).*

In the Name of the Father, Son, and Holy Spirit.

I'm preaching on Jesus' words to his disciples from today's
Gospel lesson: "No one has greater love than this, to lay
down one's life for one's friends."

On this Mother's Day, I am reminded that a loving mother is
one of the most powerful examples of what laying down your
life for someone else looks like. Mothers begin laying down
their lives for their kids during pregnancy. Even the most
empathetic dads will never know what that's like—having
another human being living inside of you for *nine months*—
every second, minute, hour, day, for *nine months.* And not
only is another human being living inside you, he or she is
growing as well. And then there's giving birth. Until the

advent of modern medicine it was not uncommon for mothers to die in childbirth, to literally lay down their lives for their babies. Again, dads can offer the occasional ice chip, but they will never have a clue about what labor and delivery actually feel like.

And pregnancy and birth are just the beginning of a mother's death for her children. Soon come the years and years of loving care—of hygiene and cooking and taxiing, the laundry and field trips and back-to-school lists and team mom chores and the PTA, and more hygiene and cooking and packing lunches and navigating demonic behavior and hormonal insanity…it never stops.

Honestly, motherhood seems to me the most important and most difficult job in the world. Motherhood involves laying down your life for your family. There is nothing metaphorical or figurative about it. It is also the most stressful job. On our refrigerator at home there is a magnet with the following request from a stressed out mom: "I'll have a café mocha vodka valium latte to go, please!"

Mothers often feel unappreciated. Mary Chapin Carpenter's "He Thinks He'll Keep Her" (1992) describes this:

> She makes his coffee, she makes his bed
> She does the laundry, she keeps him fed
> When she was twenty-one she wore her mother's lace
> She said 'forever' with a smile upon her face
> She does the car-pool, she PTA's
> Doctors and dentists, she drives all day
> When she was twenty-nine she delivered number
>   three
> And every Christmas card showed a perfect family
>
> Everything runs right on time
> Years of practice and design
> Spit and polish till it shines
> He thinks he'll keep her…

He thinks he'll keep her

One of my favorite memories of my mom involves her coming to my rescue in the midst of a very awkward situation. When I was in eighth grade, I was riding the bus to school on a gorgeous spring Friday morning, cramming for a Latin test because I had been too busy to study the night before (*Magnum P.I.* and *The Rockford Files* were on TV—*priorities*).

We had assigned seats on the bus and sitting next to me was a kid who was nice enough but let's just say his elevator did not go to the top floor. All of the sudden this kid regurgitates his breakfast all over me—partially digested peaches, and oatmeal, and other items defying identification, covered my shirt and jeans and Latin book and backpack. I was stunned, but then he did it again. I was drenched in vomit. Some kids on the bus were laughing, others were turning green and trying not to follow suit.

Finally arriving at school, I stepped off the bus, clothes soaked with vomit and walked across the lawn toward the school. Of course I walked right by Kelly, whom I had a crush on, trying to appear nonchalant about entering school with vomit all over me. I went immediately to the office and called my mom.

She stopped what she was doing and rushed to the school. We made a trade—I gave her nasty, vomit-soaked clothes and she gave me neat, folded, clean clothes. And I ended up having a great day after all—not only did the Latin test go fine, but I got to sit next to Kelly at lunch, too. I got home and found the vomit outfit was washed and folded and waiting for me on my bed. I never forgot that.

It's no secret that mothers leave a lasting impact on their children. Sigmund Freud observed that "Someone who has been the indisputable favorite of their mother keeps for life the feeling of a conqueror." Of course the corollary is that those who do not sense their mother's favor often struggle with self-confidence and feel like the conquered.

For some people, Mother's Day is a happy celebration; for others, not so much. I read this last week in *The New York Times*:

> Not all feelings about Mother's Day fit on a Hallmark card...It is perhaps the most complicated of relationships, keeping many a therapist in business. It shapes not only who we become as people, but as parents. So much of what we do once we have children is either exactly the way we were raised or a rejection of how we were raised – but either way we are responding to our mothers (*NYT*, May 9, 2012).

Some people have loving mothers who for the most part were present, kind, supportive, nurturing. Others have mothers who often absent themselves, or who withhold affection, or who abuse. Some people have mothers who call a lot, others who never call at all.

In his 2006 book, *For One More Day*, Mitch Albom tells of Charley Benetto's longings for one more day with his mom, who had passed away years earlier. He wishes he could thank her in person for all she did for him. Charley recounts several episodes from his childhood that he calls, "Times I Did Not Stand Up for My Mother." Here is one of them:

> I am six years old. It is Halloween. The school is having its annual Halloween parade. All the kids will march a few blocks through the neighborhood.
>
> "Just buy him a costume," my father says. "They have 'em at the five-and-dime."

But no, my mother decides, since this is my first parade, she will make me a costume: the mummy, my favorite scary character.

She cuts up white rags and old towels and wraps them around me, holding them in place with safety pins. Then she layers the rags with toilet paper and tape. It takes a long time, but when she is finished, I look in the mirror. I am a mummy. I lift my shoulders and sway back and forth.

"Oooh, you're very scary," my mother says.

She drives me to school. We start our parade. The more I walk, the looser the rags get. Then, about two blocks out, it begins to rain. Next thing I know, the toilet paper is dissolving. The rags droop. Soon they fall to my ankles, wrists, and neck, and you can see my undershirt and pajama bottoms, which my mother thought would make better undergarments.

"Look at Charley!" the other kids squeal. They are laughing. I am burning red. I want to disappear, but where do you go in the middle of a parade?

When we reach the schoolyard, where the parents are waiting with cameras, I am a wet, sagging mess of rags and toilet paper fragments. I see my mother first. As she spots me, she raises her hand to her mouth. I burst into tears.

"You ruined my life!" I yell (39-40).

When Charlie is a few years older, his parents get divorced and he ends up living with his mother, who is still there for him. Charley recounts other episodes that he calls, "Times My Mother Stood Up for Me," including this one:

> I am fifteen and, for the first time, I need to shave. There are stray hairs on my chin and straggly hairs above my lip. My mother calls me to the bathroom one night after (my sister) Roberta is asleep. She has purchased a Gillette Safety Razor, two stainless-steel blades, and a tube of Burma-Shave cream.
>
> "Do you know how to do this?"
>
> "Of course," I say. I have no idea how to do it.
>
> "Go ahead," she says.
>
> I squeeze the cream from the tube. I dab it on my face.
>
> "You rub it in," she says.
>
> I rub it in. I keep going until my cheeks and chin are covered. I take the razor.
>
> "Be careful," she says. "Pull in one direction, not up and down."
>
> "I know," I say, annoyed. I am uncomfortable doing this in front of my mother. It should be my father. She knows it. I know it. Neither one of us says it.
>
> I follow her instructions. I pull in one direction, watching the cream scrape away in a broad line. When I pull the blade over my chin, it sticks and I feel a cut.

"Oooh, Charley, are you all right?"

She reaches for me, then pulls her hands back as if she knows she shouldn't.

"Stop worrying," I say, determined to keep going.

She watches. I continue. I pull down around my jaw and my neck. When I am finished, she puts her cheek in one hand and smiles. She whispers, in a British accent, "By George, you've got it."

That makes me feel good.

"Now wash your face," she says (95-96).

Most of us can relate to Charley Benetto because most of us can recall times when our mothers stood up for us and times when we did not stand up for them. And even though no mother is perfect, mothers still often show us what it looks like to love someone by laying down your life for them.

In twenty years of ministry I have observed that often mothers not only feel underappreciated and overwhelmed, they also hold themselves to utterly impossible standards. Some feel like they don't measure up because they do not have the career success of Katie Couric *and* the homemaking skills of Martha Stewart *and* the beauty of Jennifer Aniston *and* the utter cool of Lorelai Gilmore of *The Gilmore Girls*...

And there are no guarantees for mothers. Even when mothers lay down their lives for their kids, sometimes kids still resent them or blame them or get into serious trouble. Some kids break their mothers' hearts, leaving them asking themselves what they did wrong.

And then there are those whose relationship with their mother is so freighted with hurt and resentment and deep-seeded wounds that it is toxic, that the goal is simply to not become like Norman Bates of the 1960 Alfred Hitchcock film, *Psycho.*

But there is good news, not only for mothers, but for all of you: *You're off the hook.*

God did not send his Son to load you down with impossible standards or guilt because your relationships with your mother or children are strained, but to save you instead, to give you grace and absolution and love. Jesus himself said, "My yoke is easy and my burden is light" (Matthew 11:30).

Arguably the most loving mother in the Bible is Mary, the mother of Jesus. As an engaged young lady, probably in her mid- to late-teens, an angel appears to her to tell her she will be bearing none other than the Son of God. How would you respond to that? Her response demonstrates her willingness to lay down her life. "Here am I, the servant of the Lord," she tells the angel, "Let it be with me according to your word" (Luke 1:38).

There are many among Mary's family, friends, and neighbors who I am sure do not believe Mary and consider her son illegitimate (wouldn't you?). Scripture is silent about how she handles this, but I am sure Mary stands up for her son.

In keeping with Jewish law, when Jesus is eight days old, Mary and Joseph take him to the temple for his circumcision and dedication. At the temple an elderly man named Simeon—who the Bible tells us is filled with the Holy Spirit—takes the infant Jesus in his arms and blesses him. Then he looks at Mary and prophesies about Jesus' life and concludes with these words: "A sword will pierce your own soul too" (Luke 2:35).

Mary appears a few more times in the Gospel accounts—finding Jesus in the temple teaching the elders at age twelve, witnessing Jesus' first miracle in turning water to wine at a wedding, seeing Jesus on occasion preaching and teaching.

The years fly by and eventually Jesus is with his disciples at the Last Supper, telling them, "No one has greater love than this, to lay down one's life for one's friends." Later that same night Jesus is betrayed and arrested.

And the next day Mary, now in her late forties, finds herself standing at the foot of the cross, gazing up at her son and helpless to do anything to ease his suffering, because it is not allowed by the Roman soldiers who carry out the crucifixion. I wonder what she thinks as she is watching and listening to her son suffer. I wonder how she must feel as people insult him even then. Scripture, again, is silent about Mary saying anything at that point, perhaps because all she can do is cry.

No doubt when Jesus is young, Mary caresses his face and kisses his head, washes and combs his hair. And now her son's face is marred, punched by Roman soldiers, his sacred head sorely wounded, a crown of thorns dug into it, hair matted with blood and sweat. No doubt when Jesus is a baby Mary examines his tiny fingernails and toenails in those tender moments of infancy. No doubt as Jesus is a toddler Mary holds his hands as he learns to walk, and tickles his feet to make him laugh. And now nails bored into those hands and feet and a sword pierces her soul too.

And yet, in spite of all this, Mary still remains at the foot of the cross. In spite of all this Mary stands up for her son as her son by hangs for the world. No doubt Jesus knew the favor of his mother Mary, and in his death on the cross Jesus conquers the power of sin and death and hell by being himself conquered.

"No one has greater love than this, to lay down one's life for one's friends."

This is what Jesus has done on the cross for you, because he loves you. Jesus loves you so much he literally laid down his life for you. There was nothing metaphorical or figurative about it.

And through his death on the cross Jesus makes a trade with you—you give him your filthy clothes of shame and sin and guilt and resentment, and he clothes you grace and absolution and love—enough to cover you, to cover your relationship with your mother, to cover your relationship with your kids.

In other words, Jesus lets you off the hook. That is the good news of the Gospel, and even if like Charlie Benetto you want just one more day to thank your mom who has passed away, don't worry. By the grace of God, someday in heaven you'll have all the time in the world.

Amen.

THE SPIRIT HELPS
US IN OUR
WEAKNESS
Paul Simon and the Paraclete

The Spirit helps us in our weakness (Romans 8:26).

In the Name of the Father, Son, and Holy Spirit.

Each year on the Feast of Pentecost we celebrate God the Father sending the Holy Spirit, in fulfillment of Jesus' promise to his disciples at the Last Supper:

> "I will not leave you comfortless," Jesus assured them, "the Comforter, which is the Holy Ghost, whom the Father will send in my name, he shall teach you all things, and bring all things to your remembrance,

whatsoever I have said unto you" (John 14: 18, 26, KJV).

And that of course, is what happened on the morning of Pentecost, as Luke writes:

> When the day of Pentecost had come, they were all together in one place. And suddenly from heaven there came a sound like the rush of a violent wind, and it filled the entire house where they were sitting. Divided tongues, as of fire, appeared among them, and a tongue rested on each of them. All of them were filled with the Holy Spirit and began to speak in other languages, as the Spirit gave them ability (Acts 2:1-4).

Often the outpouring of the Holy Spirit is associated with power, with signs and wonders, speaking in tongues and the like. As a teenager, I attended a charismatic church, and later served on staff as a youth minister at that same church. It was not uncommon for people to raise their hands or speak in tongues during the service.

There were even revival gatherings where I served as a "catcher," which meant I would stand behind people as they were prayed for and catch them if they were "slain in the Spirit" (fell backwards because they had been touched by the Holy Spirit). I witnessed episodes of people rolling on the floor in fits of "holy laughter" or uncontrolled weeping, things that Johnny Carson would have classified as "weird and wacky stuff."

Sometimes a superiority complex grows in a charismatic congregation, the idea that, because of the presence of such charismatic phenomena, they are a "Spirit-filled" congregation whereas other congregations are not. Such pride tends to alienate hurting people. Many have been burned by charismatic churches.

I attended a Christian college where charismatic phenomena were frequent at our weekly chapel services. I remember standing in an aisle at the campus bookstore at the beginning of my first semester, syllabi in hand trying to purchase all the right books, when a lady with big 80's hair and more make-up than Tammy Faye Baker placed her hands on my shoulders and leaned right up to my face. With a crazed look in her eyes, she told me that the Holy Spirit told her to tell me that the only book I needed for college—or anything else—was the Bible, and that all other books were a waste of time. Then she wandered off, presumably Spirit-led to scare some other impressionable freshman.

Certainly the Bible *is* the most important book in the world because it is the Word of God that points us to Jesus Christ, but I remember wondering if it would help me in Statistics. There used to be a segment on *Saturday Night Live* years ago called "Deep Thoughts by Jack Handey," one of which went as follows: "Instead of having 'answers' on a math test, they should just call them 'impressions,' and if you get a different 'impression,' so what, can't we all be brothers?"

For the record, I believe the Holy Spirit does move in charismatic ways sometimes, and while I think some of the "manifestations of the Spirit" I have witnessed were contrived by troubled people, others were completely legitimate. I won't speak disparaging about such things or throw the proverbial baby out with the bath water.

But in Scripture while the power of the Holy Spirit sometimes involves charismatic phenomena, more often than not it involves comforting suffering people. We see this clearly in today's lesson from Paul's Letter to the Romans in which the Apostle tells us that "The Spirit helps us in our weakness" (Romans 8:26).

When Jesus promises his disciples at the Last Supper that the Father would send the Holy Spirit, he refers to the Holy Spirit as the *paraclete*, a Greek word translated as

"Comforter" or "Advocate" or "Helper" or "Counselor." In this sermon I'm going to focus on the Holy Spirit helping us in our weakness as our Comforter.

"I will not leave you comfortless," Jesus promises his disciples, and indeed God the Father sends the Holy Spirit to be our Comforter.

When people hurt they need to be comforted. Sometimes people know why they hurt—it may be a physical pain or disease, a spouse who is completely checked out, an oppressive boss, a financial setback, or a major disappointment. Sometimes people hurt and they don't know why. Sometimes, things may be going fine in life but they can still be seized with anxiety and doubt. The rock band REM sings simply, "Everybody hurts sometimes." Singer-songwriter Paul Simon puts it this way in his 1973 song, "American Tune":

> I don't know a soul who's not been battered
> I don't have a friend who feels at ease
> I don't know a dream that's not been shattered or
> driven to its knees
> But it's all right, it's all right
> We've lived so well so long
> Still, when I think of the road we're traveling on
> I wonder what went wrong
> I can't help it, I wonder what went wrong

As a pastor, do you know what the most useful thing in my office is? It's not my computer or books or calendar or smart phone or the pencils with the cool pirate pencil toppers on them. It's not even the coffee maker or *The Book of Common Prayer.* I swear to you, as a pastor, the most useful thing in my office is the Kleenex box. Often people simply need to cry and be comforted. Often people need a hug, need to be assured that in time everything will be eventually be all right.

The Holy Spirit is this Comforter who helps us in our weakness.

Outside of Jesus Christ, the most influential person in the history of Christianity is the Apostle Paul, who spends years planting churches throughout the Mediterranean world and whose thirteen letters comprise nearly half the books of the New Testament. Certainly Paul knows more than a little about the power of the Holy Spirit, and he witnesses many supernatural healings and other miracles.

And yet for Paul, when it comes to the Holy Spirit, his emphasis is not on how the Holy Spirit is present in signs and wonders, but in how the Holy Spirit is present to comfort us and give us *grace* in the midst of our weaknesses—again, as Paul writes to the Romans, "The Spirit helps us in our weakness" (Romans 8:26). And this idea of the Holy Spirit helping us in our weakness is not a theoretical or esoteric idea for Paul; this is where Paul experiences over and over again the grace of God in his life. For Paul, grace in weakness is where the power of the Holy Spirit and the reality of his life meet. He describes this in the following vulnerable passage from his Second Letter to the Corinthians:

> Therefore, to keep me from being too elated, a thorn was given to me in the flesh... Three times I appealed to the Lord about this, that it would leave me, but he said to me, "My grace is sufficient for you, for power is made perfect in weakness" (12:7-9).

Scholars have argued and guessed for centuries about what exactly Paul's "thorn in the flesh" is. Some think it is something physical—perhaps a speech impediment or epilepsy or arthritis—others think it is something relational—perhaps family dysfunction or opposition from those opposed to his theology. Still others think his thorn in the flesh is moral—perhaps a besetting sin or character flaw from his past. Maybe it's a chronic temptation. Paul never reveals exactly what his "thorn in the flesh" is, and no one has been able to figure it out for sure either. We can only guess. But this is a good thing, as biblical scholar Paul Barnett observes:

> It may be to our advantage not to know. The very openness of the identification allows wide possibilities of personal application to a broad range of personal suffering, which precise identification might limit (*The Second Epistle to the Corinthians*, 570).

While we do not know exactly what Paul's thorn in the flesh is, we do know that it distracted him, that it would not go away. We do know that Paul did not just pray about it, he begged God not once but *three* times that the thorn would be taken away. And God's response was, "No."

But thankfully God's response did not end there; he added, "My grace is sufficient for you, for power is made perfect in weakness."

A couple questions for you: What is the thorn in your flesh that just won't go away? What is the greatest weakness in your life? Perhaps you have begged God three times, or three hundred times, for this thorn to be taken away, but it's still there. It is in those places that the Holy Spirit wants to give you comfort and help you in your weakness. This is where Pentecost connects with your actual day-to-day life.

Many local swimming pools open this time of year and I was reminded about an incident from my childhood. When I was seven years old my family joined a local YMCA swimming pool. I was really excited but I had never been in a pool in my life, so I took swim lessons, an awkward two weeks because I towered over the four- and five-year-olds who made up most of the group. On the last day we all had the opportunity to jump off the diving board and into the deep end.

Petrified, I stood at the end of the line. I watched as every single kid in front of me scampered up the ladder and without hesitation, jumped off the diving board and swam or doggy-paddled to the ladder. Our instructor was treading water under the board to give a little help to some of the kids, but most did not need it.

My turn finally came. With sweaty palms I gripped the rails and scampered up the ladder and walked to the end of the diving board, and then froze. I couldn't do it. Then my knees started to shake, and that caused the diving board to bounce up and down faster and faster, but I was still too scared to jump. This went on for awhile. The kids and parents were lined up around the deep end, encouraging me, the swim teacher was treading water under the board, assuring me that he was there to catch me, that it would be okay, that there was nothing to be afraid of. But my knees kept shaking and the board kept bouncing and I was still too scared to jump.

I could tell you that the Holy Spirit filled me with power and I triumphantly leaped off the diving board, completing a graceful double back flip with a twist and nailing the landing with a minimal splash, that I emerged from the pool to the loud applause of everyone around the pool, to which I responded with self-deprecation, "Please... I can't take credit for this; it was the power of the Holy Spirit."

But that is not what happened. As it turned out, I just couldn't do it. After awhile I turned around, red with embarrassment, and, in deafening silence, slowly wobbled the length of the undulating diving board back to the ladder and climbed back down.

When it comes to the thorn in your flesh—where you are the weakest, the most afraid, the most vulnerable—that is where the power of the Holy Spirit meets you to give you comfort, to help you in your weakness. In other words, the Holy Spirit is with you at the end of the diving board, to give you grace and comfort even if you're too scared to jump.

In the Garden of Gethsemane moments before being betrayed, Jesus, stressed to the breaking point, begged his Heavenly Father not once, but *three times*, to let the impending cup of suffering pass. But the cup did not pass; he drank it to the dregs.

And on the cross Jesus bore every thorn in your flesh, every one, as he bore a crown of, yes, thorns. And regardless of what happens with the thorn in your side this side of heaven, in heaven there will be no thorns left at all, for anyone.

And in the meantime the Holy Spirit, the Comforter, comes to you in your weakness.
In the meantime the Spirits ministers God's grace to you at the end of the diving board.

The good news on the Feast of Pentecost is that God does not leave us comfortless. The Holy Spirit is our help and gives us grace in the places of our deepest weakness. Perhaps a "Spirit-filled" congregation is a place where hurting people receive grace and comfort from the Holy Spirit and in turn can offer comfort and grace to one another as well, a place where there are plenty of hugs and plenty of Kleenex.

Amen.

BEYOND ALL MEASURE
Impossible Grief and the Eternal Weight of Glory

So we do not lose heart. Even though our outer nature is wasting away, our inner nature is being renewed day by day. For this slight momentary affliction is preparing us for an eternal weight of glory beyond all measure (2 Corinthians 4:16-17).

In the Name of the Father, Son, and Holy Spirit.

Recently someone emailed me a list of announcements from church bulletins that probably communicated something quite different from what was intended. These are not made up; they actually appeared in church bulletins. Here are a few I particularly enjoyed:

Ladies, don't forget the rummage sale. It's a chance to get rid of those things not worth keeping around the house. Bring your husbands.

Low Self Esteem Support Group will meet Thursday at 7 PM. Please use the back door.

The sermon this morning: "Jesus Walks on Water." The sermon tonight: "Searching for Jesus."

And my favorite: *Don't let worry kill you off—let the Church help.*

"Don't let worry kill you off—let the Church help"—as funny as it is there's truth in it. The Church, like the world, is filled with people who worry—people anxious about everything: how other people perceive them, their financial stress, their marriage problems, their health problems, their family dysfunction, their report cards, their weight gain—we could go on and on.

Sometimes people ache with anxiety without being able to pinpoint any specific cause. In the Simon and Garfunkel song "America" from their masterful 1968 album *Bookends* Paul Simon sings this about a young man on a long bus ride with his girlfriend, Cathy: "'Cathy, I'm lost,' I said, though I knew she was sleeping. 'I'm empty and aching and I don't know why.'"

This anxiety is not reserved to any specific age group. Everyone gets in on the fun. I recently read Rolling Stone magazine's special edition, *The 500 Greatest Albums of All Time* and coming in at # 33 was the 1976 Ramones self-titled debut album. Singer Joey Ramone said this about the songs on that album: "Our early songs came out of our real feelings of alienation, isolation, frustration – the feelings everybody feels between 17 and 75."

And the Church can often add more anxiety. Sometimes the Church burdens the burdened with sermons about things they should either start doing or stop doing, sermons often neatly packaged with "Three Points and a Poem." Sometimes the Church inadvertently helps kill off people who worry.

My all time favorite Washington Redskin is #44 John Riggins. Maybe he was onto something when at a party back in 1985 he famously called out to Supreme Court Justice Sandra Day O'Connor, "Come on, Sandy baby, loosen up!" When it comes to anxiety and worry we probably all need to loosen up, but it's not that simple, is it? The good news is that Scripture does not turn a blind eye to anxiety.

Today I'm preaching from Paul's Second Letter to the Corinthians. Of Paul's thirteen letters in the New Testament this letter is by far his most vulnerable. Paul describes the hardships of his missionary work this way: "We are afflicted in every way, but not crushed; perplexed, but not driven to despair; persecuted, but not forsaken; struck down, but not destroyed" (4:8-9). And later in this letter Paul lays out a litany of his suffering and anxiety:

> Five times I have received from the Jews the forty lashes minus one. Three times I was beaten with rods. Once I received a stoning. Three times I was shipwrecked; for a night and a day I was adrift at sea; on frequent journeys, in danger from rivers, danger from bandits, danger from my own people, danger from Gentiles, danger in the city, danger in the wilderness, danger at sea, danger from false brothers and sisters; in toil and hardship, through many a sleepless night, hungry and thirsty, often without food, cold and naked. And, besides other things, I am under daily pressure because of my anxiety for all the churches (11:24-28).

Even the Apostle Paul was no stranger to worry and anxiety. In today's passage from his Second Letter to the Corinthians Paul specifically addresses the anxiety related to aging, and shows us that God gives us hope even there:

> Even though our outer nature is wasting away, our inner nature is being renewed day by day. For this slight momentary affliction is preparing us for an eternal weight of glory beyond all measure (2 Corinthians 4:16-17).

The bad news is that "our outer nature is wasting away." We can stem the tide of the effects of aging for a time through proper diet, exercise, dying our hair and the like, but our outer nature is still wasting away, and death still awaits us all—as the band Sons of Bill sing in their song "Santa Ana Winds:" "There ain't no skating by, we're all gonna die, no matter what the plastic surgeon told you."

Some people experience this sense of wasting away not only with their physical decline, but in being trapped in situations beyond their control—be it a miserable job or a loveless marriage or being single while not wanting to be single or unrelenting stress or some other circumstance in which they feel stuck, feel like they're wasting away. And yet God offers hope even in the midst of those places. God is still renewing our inner nature day by day.

A few weeks ago in Sunday School some of the kids from Christ Church drew pictures and wrote letters for people in prison, people who literally feel like they are stuck and wasting away. One of the prisoners wrote a heartfelt thank you note that gives us a picture of what it looks like to be outwardly wasting away while inwardly being renewed day by day. Here is part of that letter:

> Greetings in the name of Jesus, I wanted to thank you for the card of encouragement I received from your church. Thank you to the

precious child who wrote the note. It is in orange and aqua and in very neat handwriting. I have it on my picture board so I can see it each day and be encouraged...Two thousand years ago Jesus sent his disciples to preach the gospel and today your church is carrying on that commission. I've only been serving God for 6 years, 4 months and as of today, 28 days. I am a babe in Christ myself but on December 31st 2005 I had an encounter with the Holy Spirit in my cell in Memphis, Tennessee and I fell in love with Jesus and God's Holy Word. I've not been the same since... Thank you again for the card and I'll add your church to my prayers and ask God to open his storehouse of blessings and pour them out upon you. Your Brother in Christ...

The good news is that although "our outer nature is wasting away, our inner nature is being renewed day by day." In other words, the work of the Holy Spirit to minister God's love and grace to us increases more and more and more.

And the good news gets even better, for Paul continues: "This slight momentary affliction is preparing us for an eternal weight of glory beyond all measure."

Think about that for a second. All the suffering Paul mentions in 2 Corinthians—the beatings, imprisonments, shipwrecks, going without food and water, the constant opposition to the gospel, the discouragement, the anxiety— all of this he refers to merely as "this slight momentary affliction." This is encouraging because often the sufferings and difficulties in our lives often feel like anything but slight or momentary, don't they?

On June 8, 1941 C. S. Lewis gave an address at Oxford University entitled "The Weight of Glory," which was later published in a collection of essays of the same name. He beautifully describes this "weight of glory" that awaits us in heaven:

> Our lifelong nostalgia, our longing to be reunited with something in the universe from which we now feel cut off, to be on the inside of some door which we have always seen from the outside, is no mere neurotic fancy, but the truest index of our real situation. And to be at last summoned inside would be both glory and honour beyond all our merits and also the healing of that old ache.

When things are going well it is not difficult to write about "the eternal weight of glory beyond all measure," to have the hope that while our outer nature is wasting away God is renewing our inner nature day by day. But when we or a loved one is dying, when the outer nature is literally wasting away right in front of our eyes, it is quite difficult. About twenty years after he delivered his "Weight of Glory" address, C. S. Lewis watched as the outer nature of his beloved wife Joy wasted away due to bone cancer. After her death he wrote a book about his grief under the pseudonym N. W. Clerk, a book that ironically some of his friends gave him to help assuage his grief. After his death this book, entitled *A Grief Observed*, was published under C.S. Lewis' actual name. Listen to how Lewis begins:

> No one ever told me that grief felt so like fear. I am not afraid, but the sensation is like being afraid. The same fluttering in the stomach, the same restlessness, the yawning. I keep on swallowing... At other times it feels like being mildly drunk, or concussed. There is a sort of invisible blanket between the world and me.

Throughout *A Grief Observed*, Lewis, like Paul, reveals his suffering and anxiety. And he also asks the questions that always surround grief, especially the "why" questions to which we are never given answers. And yet toward the end of this book Lewis reveals his hope:

> When I lay these questions before God I get no answer. But a rather special sort of 'No answer.' It is not the locked door. It is more like a silent, certainly not uncompassionate, gaze. As though he shook his head not in refusal but waiving the question. Like, 'Peace, child; you don't understand'... There is also, whatever it means, the resurrection of the body. We cannot understand. The best is perhaps what we understand least.

That is true not only when it comes to trying to understand "the eternal weight of glory beyond all measure," but also when it comes to trying to understand the source of this hope, the source of this "eternal weight of glory"—the love of God in Jesus Christ, a love that is also "beyond all measure."

Perhaps the largest measurement of distance is the light year, used in measuring the distance between stars and galaxies. The speed of light is 186,000 miles per second. A light year is the distance traveled by light over the course of a year, or, about six trillion miles. And yet the love of God, like "the eternal weight of glory," is beyond all measure, even greater than millions of light years.

And yet our experience of the love of God tends to be episodic. There are moments when the love of God feels farther away than six trillion miles, and moments when it feels closer than our skin. There are moments when we are overwhelmed by the love of God in a prison cell and moments when we watch the outer nature of a loved one waste away, feel nothing but hurt, and ask, "Why?"

In her teaching at the women's retreat a few months ago Carey Morton, a member of Christ Church, movingly described the euphoria of experiencing love when it is present and the ache when it is not:

> Is there anything headier than the sudden presence of one we love in our sphere? Love's arrival seems (and is) a miracle of connection in which another's life runs alongside and within our own. It alters what we know to be true about ourselves; it shifts our perceptions and purposes; it makes us lose words, lose weight, lose our minds. What a glorious and terrifying surrender to the life of our hearts! And because it matters to us, because the beloved matters more than ourselves, we ache when love leaves, or when our feelings grow unanswered (*Interruptions as Invitations from God* by Carey Morton, 2/25/12).

Carey is exactly right—"We ache when love leaves," but as real as this ache is; the love of God is even more real.

The remarkably talented British singer Adele, who won 6 Grammys this year, sings about this kind of love in her moving cover of Bob Dylan's song, "Make You Feel My Love." Here are a few of the verses:

> When the rain is blowing in your face
> And the whole world is on your case
> I could offer you a warm embrace
> To make you feel my love
>
> When the evening shadows and the stars appear
> And there is no one there to dry your tears
> I could hold you for a million years
> To make you feel my love

I'd go hungry, I'd go black and blue
I'd go crawling down the avenue
There's nothing that I wouldn't do
To make you feel my love

I could make you happy, make your dreams come
    true
Nothing that I wouldn't do
Go to the ends of the earth for you
To make you feel my love

The good news of the Gospel is that even though your outer nature is wasting away, your inner spirit is being renewed day by day because of the love of Jesus Christ.

The cross of Jesus Christ reaches across the yawning light years that seem to separate you from the love of God. His death proves once and for all that there is nothing that he won't do to make you feel his love, a love beyond all measure. It is this love beyond all measure that God offers you in the places of the deepest anxiety in your life, in the places in your heart where you are empty and aching and don't know why.

It is this love beyond all measure that will one day make all the suffering of your life seem but a slight momentary affliction compared to the eternal weight of glory. And it is this love beyond all measure that will ultimately beckon you inside the door of heaven—where you will meet the Apostle Paul and Joey Ramone, and all the loved ones whose outer nature wasted away before your eyes.

And there with all of them you will forever feel the love of the One who went to the ends of the earth for you; there you will experience once and for all "the healing of that old ache."

Amen.

EVERYTHING HAS BECOME NEW
Of Earthly Fathers and a Heavenly Father

So if anyone is in Christ, there is a new creation: everything old has passed away; see, everything has become new! (2 Corinthians 5:17).

In the Name of the Father, Son, and Holy Spirit.

Our Heavenly Father is in the business of making everything new. He creates and then "re-creates" so that the old creation is not thrown away but made into a new creation. This idea of God's "re-creating" is part of what a friend of mine, Tim Laniak—a gifted scholar and seminary dean—calls a "theology of the re-prefix:"

> You can't read the Old Testament carefully without noticing the amazing redundancy of words around this theme. Words such as revive, renew, recreate, restore, reform, refresh, return, repent, redeem, repair, and rebuild. I call this the Bible's 'theology of the re-prefix.' It is evidence that God finishes what he starts. He never gives up. The God we come to recognize in both Scripture and experience is One who lovingly keeps returning to his original plan.

On this Father's Day I am preaching on this "re-creating" work of God as it pertains to your relationship with both your earthly father and your Heavenly Father.

Last week I was shopping for a Father's Day card and saw one that cracked me up. It had a green road sign on the front with two arrows on it—one arrow pointed to "Dad's Way" and the other to "The Highway"—and on the inside it read, "Thanks for always showing us the way, Dad!"

The father-child relationship has a permanent impact. That is why the father-son relationship is replete with complications in literature—from Homer's *Odyssey* to Shakespeare's *Hamlet* to Turgenev's *Fathers and Sons* to Arthur Miller's *Death of a Salesman.*

My favorite father-daughter relationship in literature is the beautiful connection between Scout Finch and her father Atticus in Harper Lee's *To Kill a Mockingbird*, a relationship Lee mirrored after her relationship with her actual father, Amasa Coleman Lee. I remember as a college student watching the classic 1962 film starring Gregory Peck and thinking, "I want to be *that* kind of father."

As a pastor one of the most common things troubled people want to discuss with me is their relationship with their father. Very few topics unearth such a wide range of emotions as the father-child relationship. It is fraught with highly emotional TNT.

When I have premarital discussions with couples, one of the topics we always discuss is their relationship with their parents, because that relationship usually—directly or indirectly—has a significant impact on the marriage-to-be. Some grooms-to-be gush over their fathers—how much they feel loved by their fathers, how their fathers taught them to shoot a free throw or bait a fishhook or throw a curve ball or tie a necktie or play a D-chord, how their fathers took them to ball games or the movies or to Dunkin' Donuts early on Saturday mornings. I have officiated several weddings where the best man is the groom's father.

And some brides-to-be gush about their fathers as well—how much they too feel loved by their fathers, how their fathers told them how pretty they were, made pancakes for them, held the door open for them, read to them and rocked them to sleep, coached their basketball team, drove them to school, always met the boy who came by to pick them up for a date, and always waited up for her to return home from that date.

Others however have shared painful things with me about their relationship with their father—how as children they felt like a nuisance, how their father was checked-out or overworked. Some have shared with me about how their fathers were simply not around, or how their father pushed them to the breaking point, always demanding more and more, better and better in everything they did.

Some have shared with me about how their fathers were verbally, emotionally or physically abusive, about growing up in a constant state of fear with a knot in their stomach that never went away.

Still others have shared with me that their father died when they were young and how they wished he could have been around to walk them down the aisle or hold his grandchildren or grow old with their mom. Others whose fathers have died have told me that they miss them so much they have imaginary conversations with them when driving alone or sitting alone in their kitchen or on a solitary walk—they ask me if I think they're crazy for doing that. Of course, the answer is "no."

When it comes to their relationship with their father, no one is emotionally neutral.

One of my favorite movies is the 1989 film *Field of Dreams*, in which Kevin Costner plays Ray Kinsella, a middle-aged farmer in Iowa who hears a voice tell him to build a baseball field, "If you build it they will come." The movie begins with a montage of photos and video with a voice over by Kevin Costner, who talks about his relationship with his father:

> My father's name was John Kinsella... He played in the minors for a year or two, but nothing ever came of it... My name's Ray Kinsella. Mom died when I was three, and I suppose Dad did the best he could. Instead of Mother Goose, I was put to bed at night to stories of Babe Ruth, Lou Gehrig, and the great Shoeless Joe Jackson. Dad was a Yankees fan then, so of course I rooted for Brooklyn. But in '58 the Dodgers moved away, so we had to find other things to fight about. We did. And when it came time to go to college I picked the farthest one from home I could find.

Later in the movie Ray forms a friendship with a reclusive writer named Terrence Mann, played brilliantly by James Earl Jones. While riding in a van Ray and Terrence have a conversation about, you guessed it, Ray's relationship with his father. "What happened to your father?" Terrence asks. Ray responds,

He never made it as a ballplayer so he tried to get his son to make it for him. By the time I was ten playing baseball got to be like eating vegetables or taking out the garbage, so when I was fourteen I started to refuse. Can you believe that? An American boy refusing to have a catch with his father? ...I never played catch with him again...When I was seventeen we had a big fight, I packed my things, said something awful, and left. After a while I wanted to come home but I didn't know how. I made it back for the funeral.

"I wanted to come home but I didn't know how"—that is a loaded statement expressing a longing many people have for a restored relationship with their earthly father, something that may or may not happen in this lifetime, something that if the father has died or if there is simply too much unresolved hurt or toxic dysfunction will probably not happen in this lifetime, and yet something that is longed for just the same.

Singer-songwriter Jackson Browne describes this longing in the masterful title track from his 1973 album *For Everyman*:

> Everybody's just waiting to hear from the one
> Who can give them the answers
> And lead them back to that place in the warmth of
>   the sun
> Where sweet childhood still dances
> Who'll come along and hold out that strong and
>   gentle father's hand?
> Long ago I heard someone say something 'bout
>   everyman

I am sure that we have the gamut of father-child relationships represented here today, that some of you have a very close relationship with your father, others have a distant or strained relationship, and still others have little or no relationship at all.

But what is our Heavenly Father like?

In the Old Testament God gave Moses a brief glimpse of his glory on Mt. Sinai: "The Lord passed before him, and proclaimed, 'The Lord, the Lord, a God merciful and gracious, slow to anger, and abounding in steadfast love and faithfulness'" (Exodus 34:6).

And as I mentioned earlier the Old Testament is also replete with the "re-prefix" aspects of the love of our Heavenly Father, who revives, renews, reforms, refreshes, redeems, repairs, recreates, restores.

At his incarnation, Jesus, in agreement with his Heavenly Father, left heaven and emptied himself of his divinity in order to be fully human. Have you ever imagined what that moment must have been like for God the Father?

In 2006 the late John Updike published a short story in *The New Yorker* entitled, "My Father's Tears," in which he describes what it was like when he left his father and headed to college:

> I saw my father cry only once. I was at the Alton train station, back when the trains still ran...I blamed it on our handshake: for eighteen years we had never had occasion for this social gesture, this manly contact, and we had groped our way into it only recently. He was taller than I, though I was not short, and I realized, his hand warm in mine while he tried to smile, that he had a different perspective than I. I was going somewhere, and he was seeing me go... He had loved me, it came to me as never before. It was something that had not needed to be said before, and now his tears were saying it.

I have no doubt that God the Father similarly shed tears as his Son Jesus Christ left heaven. And the New Testament tells us that if we want to know what our Heavenly Father is like we simply look at His Son, Jesus Christ, that "In (Jesus) all the fullness of God was pleased to dwell" (Colossians 1:19); that "(Jesus) is the reflection of God's glory and the exact imprint of God's very being" (Hebrews 1:3).

Jesus himself made this clear as on one occasion he told his disciples, "The Son can do nothing on his own, but only what he sees the Father doing; for whatever the Father does, the Son does likewise" (John 5:19); and on another occasion he simply stated, "The Father and I are one" (John 10:30).

Jesus also revealed the depth of the love of his Heavenly Father when he told a Pharisee named Nicodemus that "God so loved the world that he gave his only Son" (John 3:16).

And in his parable of the Prodigal Son Jesus reveals the depth of the unconditional love of our Heavenly Father. After the prodigal son insults his father, takes his inheritance, wastes every last dime on self-centered debauchery, in desperation he returns home and his father runs to him and embraces him and welcomes him home with hugs, kisses, and a party to end all parties.

In other words, the love of Jesus mirrors the love of his Heavenly Father.

And the answer to Jackson Browne's question, "Who'll come along and hold out that strong and gentle father's hand?" is *Jesus*, whose hands—like that of his Heavenly Father—were strong and gentle, and whose hands were nailed to a cross.

And when Jesus died on the cross he gave all of us unconditional love, total forgiveness, complete absolution, grace upon grace upon grace—to restore completely your relationship once and for all with your Heavenly Father, to make you a new creation, to make all things new.

Your relationship with your Heavenly Father has been completely restored.

Let's go back to your relationship with your earthly father. Regardless of what your relationship with your earthly father is like, because your relationship with your Heavenly Father has been completely restored, because you have been given love and grace in Jesus Christ, that love and grace can be a starting point for your relationship with your earthly father. In his powerful book *Grace in Practice* Paul Zahl states, "Through absolution and the grace of God as received by the adult child, absolution and grace can become the angle of approach to forgiven parents. This is grace, the direction of one-way love" (177).

And if you are a father like me, who in some ways has done pretty well and in other ways has failed and dropped the ball; perhaps you can give yourself a little grace as well. It couldn't hurt.

Back to the film *Field of Dreams* for a moment… at the end of the movie Ray Kinsella is watching baseball players from long ago play baseball on the field he had built on his farm. He had built it, and they had come, just like the voice had told him. And Ray sees his dad John as a young man playing catcher, and stunned, tells his wife, "I only saw him later when he was worn down by life… He has his whole life in front of him, and I am not even a glint in his eye."

Ray goes to meet his dad and after talking for awhile, asks him, "Is there a heaven?" "Oh yeah," John replies, "It's the place dreams come true." As John is walking away, Ray, choked up, finally has the opportunity to ask his dad something he never thought he'd ever be able to ask him again. "Hey, dad? You wanna have a catch?" John, also choked up, smiles and nods, "I'd like that."

The movie ends with Ray and his dad John playing catch, their relationship restored.

The good news of the Gospel is that the love and grace of Jesus Christ mirror the love and grace of our Heavenly Father, that Jesus' death on the cross has completely restored your relationship with your Heavenly Father, and ensures that someday, even if you have to wait until heaven, your relationship with your earthly father will be completely restored too.

And in heaven both you and your earthly father will see that your Heavenly Father has hands strong enough to hold the universe and gentle enough to wipe away every tear from your eyes.

Amen.

THE WAY OF GRACE
Unfulfilled Callings, Motivational Posters, and that Old Love

> *...to the praise of his glorious grace that he freely bestowed on us in the Beloved. In him we have redemption through his blood, the forgiveness of our trespasses, according to the riches of his grace that he lavished on us (Ephesians 1:6-8).*

In the Name of the Father, Son, and Holy Spirit.

I imagine most of you are familiar with the motivational posters that have an inspiring photograph with a caption underneath that is intended to motivate you to change your life. I have often seen such posters in the lobbies of banks or insurance agencies or offices, posters like *"Teamwork—* Together everyone achieves more" or *"Excellence—*some excel because they are destined to, most excel because they are determined to" or "*Attitude*—the greatest discovery of any generation is that a human being can alter his life by altering his attitude."

Such posters are fine I guess, but I prefer the hilarious "demotivation" posters from the website despair.com, which claims: "Motivational posters don't work, but our demotivational posters don't work even better." These demotivation posters include "*Belief*—Believe in yourself, because the rest of us think you're an idiot" and "*Consulting*— If you're not a part of the solution, there's good money to be made in prolonging the problem" and my personal favorite, "*Wishes*—When you wish upon a falling star, your dreams can come true—unless it's really a meteorite hurtling to the Earth which will destroy all life; then you're pretty much hosed no matter what you wish for, unless it's death by meteor."

When it comes to changing lives, motivational posters fall short, but there is something that God freely gives us that can indeed change lives: grace. In the lesson from his Letter to the Ephesians the Apostle Paul mentions the "glorious grace" of God, grace that he "lavished upon us" is in Jesus Christ" (1:6-7).

Grace is God's unmerited favor toward you. Grace means God not only loves you, he likes you. Grace means that God is for you, not against you. Grace means God completely forgives you and warmly accepts you. Grace means God fully knows you and fully loves you. Grace means God loves you regardless of accomplishments, that God loves you just as much whether you graduate *summa cum laude* or *magna cum laude* or "*Thank you, laude,*" or if you never graduate at all.

Grace is unconditional love.

And Paul tells us that in Jesus Christ God has "freely bestowed" his grace to you and "lavished" his grace upon you. The Terrence Malick film *Tree of Life* (2011) opens with a voice-over by the mother figure (played by Jessica Chastain) who contrasts "the way of nature" with "the way of grace":

> The nuns taught us there are two ways through life: the way of nature and the way of grace... Grace doesn't try to please itself— accepts being slighted, forgotten, disliked; accepts insults and injuries. Nature only wants to please itself, get others to please it too, likes to lord it over them, to have its own way... They taught us that no one who loves the way of grace ever comes to a bad end.

Think about the relationships in your life right now: can you mark out the ones operating under nature and the ones operating under grace?

In relating to yourself, the way of nature involves self-critique; it involves beating yourself up over guilt from your past, and comparing yourself unfavorably against others who appear to have it all together.

Family relationships marked by the way of nature involve bullying, withholding affection, silent treatments, unkind dinner table comments, intimidation and abuse, and lots of resentment.

Churches marked by the way of nature generally heap guilt on people. They demand that people tithe, *and* participate in small groups, *and* serve on altar guild, *and* dress appropriately for Sunday services; *and*, during all those activities, to have their acts together *and* keep quiet about the baggage they bring to the table.

What about the way of grace? In relating to yourself, the way of grace involves letting oneself off the hook, seeing experiences as gifts to be received rather than deserved, letting go of the vicious competitions that circumvent everyday life.

Family relationships marked by the way of grace involve accepting one another, in spite of the neuroses and idiosyncrasies; giving each other the patient freedom to be angry or wrong; sharing laughter and inside jokes; tenderly comforting one another when life hurts.

Churches marked by the way of grace are places where one always feels welcomed; where one is encouraged by the Gospel and sacraments; where one can bring his or her lingering questions and doubts; where one can take a deep breath among the fellowship of forgiven sinners and receive the grace of God.

In short, the way of nature *kills* while the way of grace *restores life*.

Perhaps like me, you ricochet like a pinball both internally and externally between the way of nature and the way of grace. The good news of the Gospel is that God is a gracious God, that when it comes to you, God has chosen the way of grace.

The way of grace is most clearly seen in Jesus Christ, as John wrote in the prologue to his account of the gospel, "From his fullness we have all received, grace upon grace" (John 1:16).

Mary Chapin Carpenter's remarkable album, *Ashes and Roses* (2012), includes a track entitled "Old Love" that articulates the longing for grace and unconditional love:

> I want old love, the kind that takes years
> To turn to gold, love, burnished and seared
> On the high wire, by rain, wind and sun
> With the hard times forgiven and done

I want old love, the kind that seeps in
It isn't cold, love, it's never brittle or thin
It's the long kiss, it's the curl of a sigh
Down a hallway, in the middle of the night

I want old love, the kind that can see
Through the holes, love, that lives underneath
All our false cheer, bravado and pride
Through the old fears we carry inside

I want old love, the kind that can say
What it knows, love, and what it learned on the way
In that one voice, familiar and strange
Only old love remembers your name

I want old love, the kind that holds on
When it's told, love, that all hope is gone
Against all odds, wagers and prayers
To the wall love, to the furthest somewhere

The way of grace is marked by that kind of "Old Love." The grace God gives you in Jesus Christ is marked by love that indeed sees through the old fears you carry inside. It is a love that remembers your name, that holds on when all hope is gone, a love that goes to the "furthest somewhere" in your life.

Throughout his earthly ministry Jesus showed people the way of grace. He freely bestowed grace to people; He lavished his grace upon people—to the wealthy and prestigious pillars of society, to the notorious sinners, to the poor and sick and oppressed, to the elderly, to little kids, to those in serious trouble. When Jesus fed the five thousand he lavished his grace on the crowd—everyone ate "as much as they wanted" and still the disciples "filled twelve baskets" with leftovers (John 6:11, 13).

At the Last Supper Jesus reminded his disciples again that his way is the way of grace. He welcomed them by washing their feet. He ate with them even though they were still arguing among themselves about which of them was the greatest. He instituted the sacrament of Holy Communion, taking the bread and wine and gently telling them—"This is my body, broken for you... this is my blood, shed for you for the forgiveness of sins."

In his definition of the sacraments Thomas Cranmer (1489-1556), the leading figure of the English Reformation, emphasized that sacraments demonstrate that God has chosen the "way of grace." He defined sacraments as "certain sure witnesses, and effectual signs of *grace*, and God's *good will* towards us" *(BCP*, 872).

This means when you receive Holy Communion, with empty hands you are reminded again and again—every week—that, despite the present sufferings, God's way is still the way of grace. God still freely bestows his grace to you.

And the day after the Last Supper Jesus reveals the way of grace to the fullest extent when he died on the cross at the hands of those who preferred the way of nature. Jesus accepted "being slighted, forgotten, disliked;" accepted "insults and injuries." Yet even then Jesus freely lavished grace upon those who crucified him. "Father, forgive them," he prayed, "they do not know what they are doing" (Luke 23:34).

In my opinion one of the most gifted writers and speakers about the grace of God is Brennan Manning, a former Catholic priest who has often been criticized by the finger-wagging self-righteous for his honesty about his struggles with alcoholism and his failed marriage with his ex-wife, Roslyn. Brennan's health is slipping and last year he published his final book, a swan song entitled *All is Grace*. Listen to how he vulnerably describes how the grace of God has intersected with his life:

I celebrated my seventy-seventh birthday in April. If you asked me whether what I have done in my life defines my life, I would answer, "No." That's not to diminish my sins or humble-bumble my successes. It is simply to affirm a *grace* often realized only in the winter of life. The winter is stark but also comforting. I am, and have always been, more than the sum of my deeds. Thank God... If asked whether I have fulfilled my calling as an evangelist, I would answer, "No." That answer is not guilt-ridden or shamefaced. It is to witness to a larger truth, again more clearly seen in my later days. My calling is, and always has been, to a life filled with family and friends and alcohol and Jesus and Roslyn and notoriously good sinners... If asked whether I am going gently into old age, I would answer, "No." That's just plain honest. It is true that when you are old, you are often led where you would rather not go. In a wisdom that some days I admit feels foolish, God has ordained the later days of our lives to look shockingly similar to that of our earliest: as dependent children... If asked whether I am finally letting God love me, just as I am, I would answer, "No, but I'm trying" (183-184).

Because the way of grace is so foreign to the way of nature it takes years and years to seep into our hearts, as Brennan Manning's honesty makes clear. This has certainly been the case in my life.

Several years ago on an overcast weekday in early December, I was in my office and an older and wiser clergy friend of mine called me and offered to take me to lunch. At lunch he graciously asked me how I was doing, how my family was, how the ministry was going. He did not talk about himself at all. When the check came he graciously paid for it. Then he asked me to do him the honor of allowing him to buy my family some groceries for the holidays. "Meet me at Sam's Club," he grinned.

As we were walking into the store he asked me if we had a freezer. I nodded. "Excellent!" he said. He grabbed a cart and began. I wasn't sure what to do and felt a little awkward. He took the lead and simply began asking me what my family liked—"Do you all like chicken?" "Sure." He grabbed some chicken and put it in the cart. "How about steak?" I nodded. He selected a stack of the most expensive steaks and placed them in the cart. This continued as we went up and down a few aisles—he simply asked me what my family liked and put those things in the cart. At one point he said, "Please wait here a moment, I'll be right back." A couple minutes later he returned with a second cart.

At first I was trying to be a "good steward," only selecting healthy things that we needed, but he was much more gracious than that. He threw in ice cream, cookies, snacks, beer, wine. Soon the two carts were literally overflowing. We went through the checkout line. I did not contribute a dime. I did not "do my part." My friend took care of everything. Then he helped me load it in the back of my truck. Then he smiled and hugged me and thanked me for letting him do all this. Then he left.

I sat stunned in my truck for a few minutes. I was completely blown away and I couldn't fight back the tears anymore. I remember thinking, "Who does this?" It started to rain, so I rushed home. My family and I laughed, astonished, as we unloaded my truck in the rain.

That is what the way of grace looks like. It is the good news of the Gospel, that when it comes to you, God has chosen and continues to choose the way of grace. Jesus' death assures you that because he shed his blood for you, you have been forgiven; that as Paul put it in today's passage, "In him we have redemption through his blood, the forgiveness of our trespasses, according to the riches of his grace that he lavished upon us."

This also means that, as Brennan Manning writes, "If I've learned anything about the world of grace, it's that failure is always a chance for a do-over" (162). *That* is a "motivational poster" I can relate to.

So as you continue life in a world in which the way of nature tends to be the rule, be encouraged, because God has chosen the way of grace. God is gracious beyond compare, and in Jesus Christ he has lavished grace upon you.

And God will continue to offer you carts and carts and carts of overflowing grace, so you can rest assured that at the end of your life you will be received in a new way by that Old Love of God, "the hard times forgiven and done."

Amen.

18755145R00151

Made in the USA
Charleston, SC
19 April 2013